John Donne: The Poems

ANALYSING TEXTS

General Editor: Nicholas Marsh

Chaucer: The Canterbury Tales *Gail Ashton*

Shakespeare: The Tragedies *Nicholas Marsh*

Virginia Woolf: The Novels *Nicholas Marsh*

Jane Austen: The Novels *Nicholas Marsh*

Charlotte Brontë: The Novels *Mike Edwards*

Emily Brontë: Wuthering Heights *Nicholas Marsh*

John Donne: The Poems *Joe Nutt*

Further titles are in preparation

Analysing Texts
Series Standing Order ISBN 0–333–73260–X
(*outside North America only*)

You can receive future titles in this series as they are published by placing a standing order. Please contact your bookseller or, in case of difficulty, write to us at the address below with your name and address, the title of the series and the ISBN quoted above.

Customer Services Department, Macmillan Distribution Ltd
Houndmills, Basingstoke, Hampshire RG21 6XS, England

John Donne: The Poems

JOE NUTT

First published 1999 by
MACMILLAN PRESS LTD
Houndmills, Basingstoke, Hampshire RG21 6XS
and London
Companies and representatives throughout the world

ISBN 0–333–74782–8 hardback
ISBN 0–333–74783–6 paperback

A catalogue record for this book is available
from the British Library.

This book is printed on paper suitable for recycling and
made from fully managed and sustained forest sources.

10   9   8   7   6   5   4   3   2   1
08   07   06   05   04   03   02   01   00   99

Printed in Hong Kong

Published in the United States of America by
ST. MARTIN'S PRESS INC.,
Scholarly and Reference Division
175 Fifth Avenue, New York, N.Y. 10010

ISBN 0–312–22522–9 clothbound
ISBN 0–312–22523–7 paperback

For Madeleine

Contents

General Editor's Preface

This series is dedicated to one clear belief: that we can all enjoy, understand and analyse literature for ourselves, provided we know how to do it. How can we build on close understanding of a short passage, and develop our insight into the whole work? What features do we expect to find in a text? Why do we study style in so much detail? In demystifying the study of literature, these are only some of the questions the *Analysing Texts* series addresses and answers.

The books in this series will not do all the work for you, but will provide you with the tools, and show you how to use them. Here, you will find samples of close, detailed analysis, with an explanation of the analytical techniques utilised. At the end of each chapter there are useful suggestions for further work you can do to practise, develop and hone the skills demonstrated and build confidence in your own analytical ability.

An author's individuality shows in the way they write: every work they produce bears the hallmark of that writer's personal 'style'. In the main part of each book we concentrate, therefore, on analysing the particular flavour and concerns of one author's work, and explain the features of their writing in connection with major themes. In Part 2 there are chapters about the author's life and work, assessing their contribution to developments in literature; and a sample of critics' views are summarised and discussed in comparison with each other. Some suggestions for further reading provide a bridge towards further critical research.

Analysing Texts is designed to stimulate and encourage your critical and analytic faculty, to develop your personal insight into the author's work and individual style, and to provide you with the skills and techniques to enjoy at first hand the excitement of discovering the richness of the text.

NICHOLAS MARSH

Introduction

John Donne was born some time between January and June 1572. Before we begin to study his poetry, it will be helpful to us to be aware of a few crucial features of his time and his own life.

Elizabethan England was a thriving, vital, Renaissance state: it was a world alive with energy, ambition, potential and all the danger that accompanies them. The religious turmoil of the time was particularly dangerous for John Donne because he was born into an influential Catholic family at a time when Catholics were hunted out, tortured or executed mercilessly. Guy Fawkes and the other unfortunate Gunpowder Plotters were executed in public, with a brutality difficult for the modern mind to understand, when Donne was 34. As a Catholic, then, Donne was born to danger; and his family and upbringing intensified this. One of his ancestors was Sir Thomas More, who was beheaded by Henry VIII for his refusal to acknowledge any but the Pope as head of the Church, and whose book, *Utopia*, made him one of the Renaissance's greatest humanist writers, as well as a martyr. Donne himself was educated by the Jesuits, acquiring a profound and intimate understanding of his faith. So, Donne's family upbringing prepared him to be a major combatant in the religious battles of his time.

Elizabethan law made it high treason for a Catholic priest to set foot on English soil, and a crime to harbour a priest. Since Catholics must hear Mass on Sundays and holy days, and only a priest can say Mass, this made being a Catholic impossible without risking execution. Catholics who were imprisoned were routinely tortured to death by the infamous *peine forte et dure*, and the courage of many victims became legendary. Even today names like Margaret Clitherow have enormous resonance amongst English Catholics. Donne himself came perilously close to being arrested and tortured on at least one occasion that we know of when, in 1593, his brother Henry was arrested for harbouring a suspected priest. Henry betrayed the priest under threat of torture, but died of plague in Newgate Prison soon afterwards.

During his life John Donne became an apostate, abandoning his Catholicism and adopting the Protestant faith of the state. It is not known exactly how and when Donne converted (although several poems show evidence of the process in the form of spiritual and theological conflicts), but he was ordained into the Church of England in January 1615, and became Dean of St Paul's Cathedral in 1621. The important point for us to remember, in all of this, is that religious allegiance, theological controversies and disputes, filled Donne's background and life, and animated the world around him; and that religious controversy was a matter of life or death.

The second important point to appreciate as we start to study Donne, is the effect of marriage on his life. At the age of 25, Donne had been to university, travelled, fought against Spain, returned to England and was appointed to a promising and influential diplomatic position as chief secretary to Sir Thomas Egerton. He was an ambitious young man and his career was going very well indeed. All his glittering prospects were ruined however, when he fell in love with and secretly married Anne More, Sir Thomas's niece. Donne was dismissed and sent to prison when their marriage was discovered in 1602, and his diplomatic career was over. From then on, the Donnes lived through many years of penury and dependence before he began a second career in the Church, under pressure from King James.

In 1617 Anne died in childbirth with their twelfth or thirteenth child (biographers disagree), and, although we know that Donne was devastated, we know very little else about the woman whose body and mind must have given rise to some of the most powerful love poetry ever written. After all, no man writes love poetry without experiencing love. In the epitaph he wrote for her he called her, 'A woman most choice, most beloved and most loving, a wife most dear and most chaste, a mother most pious, dutiful, self-sacrificing, and indulgent,' adding that he was at her death, *dolore infans*, 'by grief made wordless', an eloquently simple tribute.

The final point to bear in mind, before we turn to the poems themselves, is that Donne did not write for publication. Poetry was a fashionable pastime, and was considered almost a necessary part of courtship. Donne was evidently addicted to writing poetry, but he did not take his poems seriously, and they were intended for circulation among a limited group of acquaintances. Perhaps as a result of this, the poems are uncompromising and intellectually demanding. In them we will find the mind of a man fiercely engaged with the intellectual conflicts of his age, a mind energised by a vast range of subjects and ideas, and one well equipped to make sense of that disorder. Reading Donne gives us a feeling that we are reading inside the man's head. Collectively, the poems construct an identity which impresses us with its emotion, wit and intellect, but also essential human frailty. He took by the throat a form which was all balance and harmony, forcing it to swallow all the confusion and energy of his own heart and soul, until it was transformed into something more beautiful and lasting, because more honest.

PART 1

ANALYSING JOHN DONNE'S POETRY

1

Elegies and Lust

In this chapter we will look at a number of poems which exhibit an uninhibited, imaginative pursuit of sexual experience. The following elegy, *To his Mistris going to Bed*, was considered indecent enough to be omitted from the first printed edition of his poetry after his death, but manuscript evidence places it firmly before 1599 so we can ascribe it to Donne's early twenties. For ease of use as we begin our study, it is quoted in full.

Elegie XIX, To his Mistris going to Bed

Come, madam, come, all rest my powers defie,
Until I labour, I in labour lie.
The foe oft-times having the foe in sight,
Is tir'd with standing though he never fight.
Off with that girdle, like heavens Zone glistering,   5
But a far fairer world incompassing.
Unpin that spangled breastplate which you wear,
That th'eyes of busies fooles may be stopt there.
Unlace your self for that harmonious chyme,
Tells me from you, that now it is bed time.   10
Off with that happy busk, which I envie,
That still can be, and still can stand so nigh.
Your gown going off, such beautious state reveals,
As when from flowry meads th'hills shadow steales.
Off with that wyerie Coronet and shew   15
The haiery Diademe which on you doth grow;

7

Now off with those shooes, and then safely tread
In this loves hallow'd temple, this soft bed.
In such white robes, heaven's Angels us'd to be
Receaved by men; Thou Angel bringst with thee   20
A heaven like Mahomets Paradice; and though
Ill spirits walk in white, we easly know,
By this these Angels from an evil sprite,
Those set our hairs, but these our flesh upright.
    Licence my roaving hands, and let them go,   25
Before, behind, between, above, below.
O my America! my new-found-land,
My kingdome, safeliest when with one man man'd.
My myne of precious stones, My Emperie,
How blest am I in discovering thee!   30
To enter in these bonds, is to be free;
Then where my hand is set, my seal shall be.
    Full nakedness! All joyes are due to thee,
As souls unbodied, bodies uncloth'd must be,
To taste whole joyes. Gems which you women use   35
Are like Atlanta's balls, cast in mens views,
That when a fools eye lighteth on a Gem,
His earthly soul may covet theirs, not them.
Like pictures, or like books gay coverings made
For lay-men, are all women thus array'd;   40
Themselves are mystick books, which only wee
(Whom their imputed grace will dignifie)
Must see reveal'd. Then since that I may know;
As liberally, as to a Midwife, shew
Thy self: cast all, yea, this white lynnen hence,   45
Here is no pennance, much less innocence.
    To teach thee, I am naked first; why then
What needst thou have more covering than a man.

A first reading tells us that the poet is far from shy. Donne revels
in the business of undressing his mistress in stages, his excitement
mounting as she acquiesces until the climactic exclamation, 'Full
nakedness!' (l. 33). His desire recognises few limits and he urges the
girl on with:

Licence my roaving hands, and let them go,
Before, behind, between, above, below.

(ll. 25–6)

The same explicitness is evident in his wish:

As liberally, as to a Midwife, shew
Thy self:

(ll. 44–5)

Evidently he feels no compunction to be decorous. This points towards a fundamental fact we need to appreciate about Donne's love poetry: that this type of verse was written for a very limited coterie of friends. It would not have been written with any kind of publication in mind. In fact, Donne openly decried his own poetry as trivial and insignificant, and kept few copies of his poems.

Returning to the poem, we should notice that a first reading gives us a clear idea of the subject (a girl undressing) and the speaker's mood (lust). Our immediate response, then, is not difficult or confused. On the other hand, if we look at the opening four lines of this poem, we can see that it resists easy interpretation. Donne proclaims his excited state openly via two puns, on 'labour' and 'standing'. Puns are less common in the present than they were in Donne's time, bombarded as we are with immediate visual imagery; but verbal games were the essence of good taste then, and we need to grasp that to enjoy the verse of the age. Today, the word 'wit' refers to the colloquial quips people employ as common currency, most of which would be better described as sardonic. In Donne's time, however, 'wit' meant something much more than this. In this study we will use the term 'wit' to describe the entire range of verbal games Donne plays with his reader. In this more meaningful sense, wit not only enlightens, it also challenges the reader on deeply difficult matters.

What of Donne's opening puns? Until he labours in making love to the girl, he has to endure a different kind of labour, and this is where we need to appreciate that Donne is paying us a compliment, expecting us to think of additional meanings such as 'labouring in vain', 'hard labour', or even the struggle to proceed on a journey of some kind, and then the pun works. Note also how compact the line is. Not a word is wasted and from this tautness springs a far richer meaning. Again this is something we will find is characteristic of Donne. The briefest of images can sometimes blossom into the most complex thoughts, particularly when we think about them in the context of the whole poem. The second pun, on 'standing', compares Donne 'standing' to watch his mistress undress with a soldier 'standing' waiting for a battle to begin; but the pun additionally relies on us to link 'standing' with the poet's erect penis. The analogy between seduction and preparing for battle has a long history, and Donne jokes here that if he has to wait much longer he will be too tired to fight.

Having proclaimed his intent, Donne then issues a number of commands for the girl to remove various items of her clothing. The technical unfamiliarity of some of them should not disturb us, but we need to know that a 'busk' (l. 11) is a stiff corset, and its closeness and unique postioning are what Donne envies. Yet is that all? A closer look at the lines concerned:

> Off with that happy busk, which I envie,
> That still can be, and still can stand so nigh.
>
> (ll. 11–12)

reveals another pun. We may notice the pun here because 'still' is quickly repeated, as 'labour' was in line 2. This will prove a helpful way of picking up double meanings in Donne's poetry. So, how does the pun on 'still' work? We need to look at what Donne says about the girl following each of the items she removes. One example will serve. Though her girdle is 'like heavens Zone glistering' (l. 5) she is 'far fairer' (l. 6). What Donne stresses is her beauty. The function of the breastplate she wears is not to adorn her, but to prevent men ogling her she is so beautiful. This hyperbolic tone, applied to the girl, persists throughout the poem, and is a conventional technique in Renaissance love poetry, most famously parodied by Shakespeare in his *Sonnet CXXX*, *My mistress' eyes are nothing like the sun*.

So beautiful is Donne's 'mistris', that were he to replace the busk,

physically become that intimate with her, he could never remain
still. Nor, we imagine, could he 'stand' still, and in that case he
would soon not still 'stand'. It is a rich and amusing pun which
nonetheless praises her beauty.

Continuing his undressing, Donne produces the lovely compli-
ment:

> Your gown going off, such beautious state reveals,
> As when from flowry meads th'hills shadow steales.

(ll. 13–14)

one of the few genuinely sensuous images in the poem, before
coming to a more conventional image which nonetheless, requires
further consideration:

> In such white robes, heaven's Angels us'd to be
> Receavd by men; Thou Angel bringst with thee
> A heaven like Mahomet's Paradice; and though
> Ill spirits walk in white, we easly know,
> By this these Angels from an evil sprite,
> Those set our hairs, but these our flesh upright.

(ll. 19–24)

Calling the girl an 'angel' is nothing new, but Donne's angel brings
with her 'Mahomets Paradice'. It is a difficult phrase. Firstly we must
remember that Donne was born and educated a Catholic and as
such he could hardly use the word 'angel' carelessly. Secondly, having
established the metaphor, he is quick to generate the joke involving
the word 'set', where evil spirits in white robes are distinguishable
from 'angels' like the girl, because they make our hair stand on end,
while she gives him an erection. (This use of one word, 'set' to act
for two different nouns, is technically called syllepsis.) The juxtapo-
sition of paradise, a Christian heaven, with this indecency would
have been tasteless, and to avoid it Donne equates her paradise with
Mohammed, and therefore renders it safely exotic. The Muslim par-
adise, for a Christian of the period, was a place of very earthly
delights, most of them sexual.

From here Donne's excitement mounts. The rhythm of the prepositional list in line 26, imitates the excited movements we might imagine as she acquiesces to his wish. The exclamation, 'O my America!' underlines this excitement and is followed by more clever wordplay, 'one man man'd,' 'My myne'. What follows is absolutely characteristic of Donne. 'To enter in these bonds, is to be free' (l. 31) is a dramatically obvious paradox. The reader is again included in the text by being forced to resolve the paradox. Donne can only be free in the girl's arms, by being enslaved to her. And look at 'discovering' (l. 30) to see just how densely Donne plays with words. The paradox is then continued into the last line of this section where notions of setting one's seal to a legal document, or 'bond', are applied directly both to Donne's wish to be the girl's lover, and his physical actions as he imagines himself making love to her.

We should consider the whole poem at this point. If Donne's aim was to seduce, he appears to have succeeded. But this is to underestimate Donne's poetic confidence. The coaxing moves onto an outrageously daring level: lines 34–5 suggest that, just as souls must depart bodies if eternal joy in heaven is to be gained, so must bodies give up clothes if sexual joy is the object. But there follows an odd diversion. The caesura in line 35 at 'joyes', abruptly halts all progress and Donne proceeds with a classical allusion, to liken jewellery worn by women to the golden apples Hippomenes threw to divert Atalanta's attention in the running race which gained him her hand and saved his head. Donne argues that the 'fools' who are diverted by such things cannot distinguish between the woman herself and her possessions; and in another analogy to books, and then covers, he characterises the 'fools' as 'lay-men' who are not permitted to read (or are illiterate and so cannot read) the 'mystique books' of this faith. These analogies, and the diction Donne uses, imply a hyperbolic compliment both to the girl and to himself. She is treated as a religious object, and one so sacred that only high priests may approach it. He, on the other hand, is a high priest who has the perfect faith and authority to read her 'mystique book'. A further compliment to women explains that Donne will be 'dignified' by the 'grace' he receives from knowing her. Another caesura at this point gives time for breath before the long-sought-after wish is voiced:

Must see reveal'd. Then since that I may know;
As liberally, as to a Midwife, shew
Thy self:

(ll. 43–5)

The abrupt caesura in line 43 alerts us, so that we cannot miss the daring of Donne's conclusion: at the culmination of several lines dominated by classical and sacred imagery, the poet suddenly brings us back to frank physical reality. The phrase 'as to a Midwife', crowns Donne's elaborate compliment with earthy directness, an extraordinarily daring effect.

We may be confused, at the end of the poem, that Donne refers to 'this white lynnen' (l. 45), when 'full nakedness' came earlier. However, this becomes clearer when we realise that the girl was still wearing jewellery and an undergarment at this point. The jewellery goes first, which prepares the way for Donne to demolish the last of her moral reservations, asking her to cast aside her final pretence with the final garment. 'Here is no pennance, much less innocence', he asserts, sustaining the duality of the poem's focus, simultaneously on abstract ideas and physical garments, right to the end.

It only remains for Donne in his eagerness, to show the girl the way and leave us with one final humorous image which exudes the same confidence and strength exhibited throughout the poem:

To teach thee, I am naked first; why then
What needst thou have more covering than a man.

(ll. 47–8)

However, before we leave this poem and look at less frivolous work, we should consider what it can tell us about Donne's love poetry. He had little time for the chivalrous poetry which was plentiful in Elizabethan England, and was always conscious of his own uniquely rough voice. We might ask ourselves, what is the function of a love poem? We might reflect for a moment on other love poetry we have read. We can start by considering the girl in this poem. What does she look like? What is her background? Her garments suggest she is a member of the court, which would accord with the convention of Renaissance love poetry. Yet who is she? She is very beautiful, we know that, but is she blonde or dark: tall or short? It is an easy point to make. Donne does not tell us what she looks like; nor does the poem primarily aim to brag or titillate. What Donne is most interested in is what he can do with words. How far can he go in praising, coaxing, persuading? What shocking arguments and inventive images he can adduce to his cause? We will see as we continue this study that no matter how sensual the subject matter, Donne is always provoked to think.

We have used this first poem as a sample: analysing it has helped us to recognise some characteristics of Donne's poetry, and to identify some techniques and approaches which are useful when studying his verse. It is worth stopping at this point to summarise what we have learned, so we can apply this to future analyses.

First, we found that the overall subject-matter and purpose of the poem was clear from a first reading; but that understanding this did not help us in the way we might expect. This poem, about seduction and sex, has surprisingly little sensual imagery or physical description. It was necessary to clarify Donne's ideas in our minds, stage by stage, starting at the beginning of the poem and following the development of his thought. At certain points, it was helpful to step back and consider our detailed understanding in relation to the overall purpose of the poem. This helped us to see how Donne goes beyond mere seduction: the poem has a larger purpose, to develop and pursue his ideas to a pitch of daring and originality which challenges us to re-evaluate our own thoughts.

Secondly, we noticed puns and dense word play, often highlighted by the repetition of a word. We are expected to think of various alternative meanings, and try them all out in the context of the poem: in this way we heighten our awareness of ambiguities, paradoxes and other forms of multiple meaning as Donne's ideas develop.

Thirdly, we have found Donne's images and analogies come from widely different sources and are often brought together daringly in ways we do not expect. For example, at the end of the poem, ideas of religious worship, sin, penitence and frank physical sexuality are combined in an almost shocking conclusion. Certainly, religious, romantic and sexual ideas are all brought into service at the same time.

The second poem we will analyse in this chapter is *Elegie* XVIII, *Love's Progress*. We have some way to go before we can say we have dealt confidently with Donne at his most difficult, but even this poem represents a step up in the demands it makes on the reader. If we find ourselves puzzled or confused, it is a helpful step to pay strict attention to each sentence as a single unit. That way we can usually follow Donne's often convoluted line of reasoning. An initial reading should establish the connection with *To his Mistris going to Bed*. Like the former poem, this one takes as its central concern sexual love, ending on a note of sententious advice for the 'Who ever loves' who begins the poem. Put simply, sex is 'the right true end of love'. Of course Donne is far more interested in how he reaches that conclusion than the conclusion itself, so it falls to us to trace at least part of that journey.

The up anchor is fairly simple. Whoever loves, Donne says, and does not aim at the 'right true end' is like someone who goes to sea for no other purpose but to be sick. The idea of love as a sea journey is set, but Donne delays his daring exploration for later, although having read the poem we might be tempted to rush on ourselves. Like a bear licking its cub too eagerly, we can turn love into a mis-shapen monster. A calf born with a man's head might be better than a calf because more human, but is nonetheless monstrous. 'Perfection is in unitie' Donne asserts, meaning something akin to purity of design. If the argument seems a little strained, then thinking of moving from freaks of nature to perfect examples of nature's creation should help us. Donne is urging us on to seek perfection:

> Perfection is in unitie: preferr
> One woman first, and then one thing in her.
>
> (ll. 9–10)

The next six lines provide us with a further example to firm up his argument. Gold, one of Donne's favourite images, is rare and unique in several ways, but its true value lies in our employment of it as 'the soul of trade' (l. 16). The word 'soul' should immediately trigger our awareness. We should remember Donne's background and the fiercely religious nature of the society in which he was a key figure, and value the word accordingly. This is a powerful association for Donne, and by implication we are led to think where he might now locate the 'soul' of woman. Women *may* have many qualities, he continues, but we should love only one. What greater hurt can man give woman than to love her for some inessential quality, some peripheral aspect of her femininity?

'Makes virtue woman?' asks Donne, abruptly leaping at the foe. This kind of compact expression, which omits words, is called ellipsis. It can be difficult for the reader, but we can easily understand by stopping for a moment to think it out in full. If we try to write it out at length, 'Makes virtue woman?' becomes 'Is virtue the only thing that makes a woman a woman?' Now we have Donne's idea clearly stated, and can continue with the poem. However, it is important to complete the process of study by looking back to the poem. Our long version is clear, but it is clumsy and unattractive. Donne's three words are compact, sudden and hard-hitting, and it is this effect of tense, hurrying vigour that we want to keep with us as we read on. Immediately we find another example of condensed grammar, which again demands our attention before we are sure of the sense:

> Makes virtue woman? must I cool my bloud
> Till I both be, and find one wise and good?

> (ll. 21–22)

The tone seems impatiently angry ('must I . . . ?') and Donne is clearly unwilling to wait until he finds a woman who is both 'wise and good'. However, it takes us longer to understand the phrase 'Till I both be', because we have to ask what Donne's verb 'be' refers to? In this situation try the same technique again, paying attention to where the comma is placed. Here is a full version of what leads up to the comma: 'Is virtue the only thing that makes a woman a woman?

and must I keep myself restrained until I can be both (virtuous and restrained)?' This makes it clear that 'be' refers backwards, as it must because the comma separates it from the rest of line 22, so 'both' must mean the two qualities the poet has just mentioned: virtue, and coolness or restraint. The rest of the line then presents no problems: all we need to do is supply a few obvious words to fill out the sense: '*and until I can find one woman who is both wise and good?*'

Now we understand these lines, but again we should complete the work by looking back at Donne's words, to appreciate the poet's effect. In the poem, the two short verbs 'be' and 'find' are very close together: they are like a central pivot for the idea. These two active words refer backwards for two qualities (virtue and coolness) and forwards for two (wisdom and goodness). This structure pulls all the ideas in the sentence together into the middle, where the verbs are. We could speculate that the way this works is to emphasise the effort that would be needed to assemble all these qualities in a couple. Just as it seems to take impossible grammar, it would take impossible effort to find two good people, one of each sex. Donne is clearly not willing to wait that long.

The technique we have just used for unravelling complex syntax, seems very time-consuming and unwieldy when we explain and detail each stage. Most of the techniques we use to analyse texts are like this, however, and you should not be put off using them. Begin by tackling the dense and complex parts of a poem in this way, and you will be surprised how quickly you are able to see the meaning, without having to drudge through each stage of the method. Soon, you will work out Donne's grammar, and fill out ellipses by adding the missing words, almost automatically, so that it does not consume your time. The important stage to remember is the final one, when you put Donne's poem back together and appreciate the effect he achieves when he compresses so much thought into so few words.

It's worth repeating that some difficulties of interpretation can be relatively easily overcome by reading with the sentence as a unit in mind. A number of astute literary minds have worked long and hard on editing Donne's poetry and it would be foolish of us to ignore their skilful punctuation.

The caesura in line 22 allows Donne to recollect himself a little and suggest that when we love a woman, it is not virtue, or beauty, or even wealth which is at her heart, or by the earlier implication, her soul. The man who loves solely for one of these is as adulterous, Donne states, as he who seduces her maid. Though this might outrage modern feminine sensibilities, we mustn't let it stand in the way of the poem. Search in the heavens and we will still not find love's proper end, 'our *Cupid*', because he lies underground. This positioning of love with the God of the Underworld, Pluto, and the accompanying images of fire and gold, allows Donne to make the major point he has been preparing for and which he is eager to elaborate:

> Men to such Gods, their sacrificing Coles
> Did not in Altars lay, but pits and holes.
> Although we see Celestial bodies move
> Above the earth, the earth we Till and love:
> So we her ayres contemplate, words and heart,
> And virtues; but we love the Centrique part.

(ll. 31–36)

It is the kind of shocking, daring leap of the imagination which earned the displeasure of critics like Samuel Johnson. Donne has leapt from the idea of Cupid belonging underground, to the image of the vagina as 'pits and holes' via the suspect notion that men sacrifice to such Gods not on altars, but on the earth itself. Yet there is something else we should consider before we condemn him too readily. Although we might admire the heavens, it is the earth we love and 'Till'. His emphasis on fertility and procreation raises the 'Centrique part' to something more like the womb than the vagina.

Nonetheless, the point has been made and Donne is quick now to embark on the rich journey which he has delayed since the poem began. Declaring, equally daringly, that the 'womb' is every bit as infinite as the soul because fertile, he now denounces those who seek sex by beginning at the woman's face. Safely on board, he sails downwards from the woman's hair, across her brow, nose, eyes like suns, cheeks, to her lips where we 'anchor' and 'think our selves at home' (l. 54). The journey is a mixture of classical allusion and contemporary exotica '(Not faynte Canaries, but Ambrosiall)' and Donne relishes the jokes on the way, repeatedly intimating at woman's unpredictability and capacity for giving joy and misery. From the lips we hear 'Syrens songs' and 'Delphick Oracles' while the 'cleaving tongue' becomes 'The Remora,' a sucking fish which in Donne's day had a mythological ability to cling to ships and slow their passage.

Crossing the 'boundless sea' of her stomach, we sail on towards 'her *India*,' her vagina, which again employs the exotic to emphasise the adventurous, almost heroic nature of the journey. It is worth while contemplating for a moment how arduous and almost magical, a trip to India would have been for an Englishman in James I's court. By this time we are carried headlong by our passion, the current becomes our Pilot, but Donne warns us of the dangers of the vulva, and pubic hair in which many unfortunate sailors appear to drown. However amusing we find this, he is intent on more than humour:

> Though thence the Current be thy Pilot made,
> Yet ere thou be where thou wouldst be embay'd,
> Thou shalt upon another Forest set,
> Where many Shipwrack, and no further get.

(ll. 67–70)

The joke is quickly followed by a reminder of just how gloriously worthwhile this journey is:

> When thou art there, consider what this chace
> Mispent by thy beginning at the face.

(ll. 71–72)

If there is something offensive about this, a crudeness which seems intent on denying the individuality of the woman concerned, we should call to mind two points. One we have already learned from *Elegie* XIX. It is unusual to find Donne dealing with a flesh and blood individual. We will not find anything remotely like Petrarch's Laura, or Shakespeare's Dark Lady in Donne. Secondly, the *Elegies* and the *Satyres* belong to Donne's early years as a fashionable young man in Lincoln's Inn, in the company of other fashionable young men. Donne may have had to live with the added anxiety and danger of being a Catholic, but he was after all flesh and blood, and had probably seen enough real flesh and blood spilt in martyrdom and war to relish living and loving.

Having chastised his reader for a misguided fascination with faces, he moves on to suggest a better route, beginning with the foot. We could argue at length about what possible 'Symetry' Donne believed he had discovered between the foot and the vagina but it is more likely that it is contrariness which appeals to him. If most men start at the face, Donne is going to start at the foot, and justify doing it too. Using the Devil's foot as his model of immutability, he assures us that the foot represents 'Firmness' and is after all 'the first part that comes to bed'. If from civility we kiss hands, knees and even the 'Papal foot', and if kings find nothing objectionable in that, who are lovers to disagree?

> For as free Spheres move faster far than can
> Birds, whom the air resists, so may that man
> Which goes this empty and Aetherial way,
> Than if at beauties elements he stay.

(ll. 87-90)

If we have stressed before the youthful nature of this poetry, we can see it here again where Donne uses the heavenly spheres which move at incalculable speed compared to the birds which struggle against the air, as ideals to mimic. Speed of seduction, how quickly we can get ourselves 'embay'd' (l. 68), is evidently more important than anything else.

The final justification for this curious journey relies on another pun. Donne plays wittily with the word 'purses', evoking it both as a noun and as a verb. If we analyse this final image, we can again see how challenging Donne's verse can be to readers with modern tastes and expectations:

> Rich Nature hath in women wisely made
> Two purses, and their mouths aversely laid:
> They then, which to the lower tribute owe,

That way which that Exchequer looks, must go:
He which doth not, his error is as great,
As who by Clyster gave the Stomack meat.

(ll. 91–6)

Nature has endowed women with two mouths, or 'purses', and these are 'aversely laid'. The adverb implies opposition, as though not only are a woman's mouth and vagina physically disparate, they are somehow opposed in intent too. Is Donne evoking the conventional masculine image of woman as untrustworthy and paradoxical? saying one thing but meaning another? A purse in Donne's day was also a loose bag, usually of leather, with a string to draw it tight. Does this affect our response to either the woman's mouth or her vagina? Does the invitation to think of pursing lips, enhance or vulgarise the woman's appeal? Whatever our response, we cannot avoid the conclusion Donne reaches. 'Who ever loves', and knows 'the right true end of love', has come to the same conclusion, and pays tribute to the appropriate place, the vagina. Sexual union is the proper end of love. He who denies this is like a man trying to feed himself by giving himself an enema or 'Clyster'.

However we react to this crudely limited view, whatever our own gender, we should not lose sight of the two fundamental points we have gleaned from both poems analysed so far. Although we might wish to call these poems love poems, they are so in a restricted sense. Even on a potentially titillating journey, in which almost every detail of a woman's anatomy is toyed with and relished, Donne appears disinterested in appealing to our senses. Can we find any image in *Loves Progress* that strikes us as sensual or exciting?

As in *To his Mistris going to Bed*, there is no flesh-and-blood, identifiable woman reading this poem and being seduced by it. Donne is writing something to amuse his friends, a literary game which stimulates his intellect more than his sexual desire.

Just how vibrantly and startlingly the experience of love could stimulate Donne's mind, can be seen if we turn now to one of his more justifiably famous poems, *Aire and Angels*, which is quoted in full.

Before reading it we should appreciate the significance of angels
in Donne's world because it goes vastly deeper than a conventional
compliment about physical beauty. He writes about them constantly
and they clearly fired his imagination. As a Catholic, Donne knew a
lot about angels, and was extremely well read on theological matters.
In an age when religious controversy permeated every aspect of life,
it was impossible to be educated and not take part in that contro-
versy, at the very least internally. He took his ideas about angels
largely from the writings of St Thomas Aquinas which meant that to
him angels were paradoxically incredibly powerful, yet possessed no
physical body at all. They were unknowable in material terms, some-
where between God and man, yet ultimately mysterious. They also
possessed a unique ability to adopt a body of pure air just sufficient
to enable them to function on earth, but not substantial enough for
us to view them. What is certain, we should not doubt the strength
of his belief in their existence. As the child of a powerful English
Catholic family, Donne received expert tuition from the Jesuits and
would have been well versed in angels and their various spiritual
capacities.

Therefore, when we read *Aire and Angels,* we must make the effort
to feel with him the weight of the comparisons he makes. We should
also note before we start, that our advice to concentrate on the sen-
tence as a unit might be severely strained here. This is Donne at his
most complex and demanding and the whole poem employs only
three sentences. Nevertheless, we should make every effort to keep
hold of the structure of those sentences as we read.

Aire and Angels

Twice or thrice had I loved thee,
Before I knew thy face or name;
So in a voice, so in a shapelesse flame,
Angells affect us oft, and worship'd bee;
    Still when, to where thou wert, I came,   5
Some lovely glorious nothing I did see.
    But since my soule, whose child love is,
Takes limmes of flesh, and else could nothing doe,
    More subtile than the parent is,

Love must not be, but take a body too,   10
    And therefore what thou wert, and who,
        I bid Love aske, and now
That it assume thy body, I allow,
And fixe it selfe in thy lip, eye, and brow.

Whilst thus to ballast love, I thought,   15
And so more steddily to have gone,
With wares which would sinke admiration,
I saw, I had love's pinnace overfraught,
    Ev'ry thy haire for love to work upon
Is much too much, some fitter must be sought;   20
    For, nor in nothing, nor in things
Extreme, and scatt'ring bright, can love inhere;
    Then as an Angell, face, and wings
Of aire, not pure as it, yet pure doth weare,
    So thy love may be my loves spheare;   25
        Just such disparitie
As is twixt Aire and Angells puritie,
'Twixt womens love, and mens will ever bee.

We can now begin the detailed analysis, hopefully without deconstructing any of its considerable elegance and grace, but it will require considerable imput from us as readers. As we have noted, Donne tends to stimulate, not patronise, his reader. He opens the poem by describing the curious experience common to people in love, the idea that this individual is, and has always been, the perfect partner for them. It is as though we know of them before we ever meet them:

> Twice or thrice had a I loved thee,
> Before I knew thy face or name;

(ll. 1–2)

When we do, we feel a strange confirmation of that previously half-felt knowledge. As men know of angels only through their mysterious communications:

> So in a voice, so in a shapelesse flame,

(l. 3)

so we know of the one true love. And of course, both are 'worship'd'. Yet when Donne actually meets the girl, he still finds her too insubstantial, too ethereal, too magnificent and unreachable:

> Some lovely glorious nothing I did see.
>
> (l. 6)

The first six lines not only form the first sentence, but their abbaba rhyme pattern links them coherently by sound too. The tone is gentle, reflective. There is nothing to jar or disturb us, until the bathotic (anticlimactic) surprise of 'nothing' in line six.

There follows an argument we should be familiar with already from *Loves Progress*, 'May barren Angels love so' (l. 23). Donne argues that since his soul has a physical body, 'Takes limmes of flesh, and else could nothing doe', and love is the child of his soul, Love must also take a physical shape, 'Love must not be, but take a body too', and so he comes to recognise and love her physically. 'And fixe it selfe in thy lip, eye, and brow' (l. 14). It is the same debate which takes so much time and energy in *Loves Progress*. Without sex there is no love.

But if we now reread the last verse of the poem, we should find that something more complicated and elevating is being suggested. It helps us to know that a 'pinnace' (l. 18) is literally a small boat, but was, figuratively, a colloquialism applied to women.

In seeking to maintain his equilibrium, 'to ballast love,' he discovers he has gone too far – we assume, in expressing that love – and unbalances the very love he wishes to keep safe. The imagery revolves, throughout these lines, around boats and freight, where both the literal and figurative meanings of 'overfraught' (l. 18) are being played on. It seems the intensity of his love, 'Every thy haire for love to work upon' is too much for the girl, and indeed for Donne himself, so that 'some fitter must be sought' (l. 20). Love cannot find its permanent, essential home in 'nothing,' or in the extremity or brilliance of passion or beauty:

> For, nor in nothing, nor in things
> Extreme, and scatt'ring bright, can love inhere;
>
> (ll. 21–2)

It requires something even rarer, unique, to keep it secure and stable. Donne finds this quality via his theological knowledge of angels. Just as angels adopt a body of pure air, which although less pure than the angels themselves, is still purer than humanly comprehensible, so the girl's love may adopt the same relationship to Donne's and become, 'my loves' spheare'. The spheres of Elizabethan cosmology were thought to each have a guardian angel of their own. At this point we face some extremely difficult questions. A survey of past critical readings of the poem shows that Donne's three-line conclusion causes all sorts of dilemmas and problems of resolution. One view has been to find a dissatisfying and abrupt shift of tone, from the sincere voice of a love, expressing itself elegantly, to a tone in which Donne returns to the misogynistic views he expresses elsewhere – what John Carey in his comprehensive study calls, 'a cheap crack about the inferiority of woman's love to man's'.[1] Others have tried to ignore the implication behind the word 'puritie,' and insist that its use is limited to the difference between angels' real forms and their body of air forms.

What we should first note is that an abrupt ending is extremely characteristic of Donne. We will meet it repeatedly in our analyses and suggested reading. He was undoubtedly fond of shifting tone in a dramatic fashion in either the final couplet, or final few lines of his poetry. Yet is that what is happening here?

> Just such disparitie
> As twixt Aire and Angells puritie,
> 'Twixt womens love, and mens will ever bee.

> (ll. 26–8)

Taken in isolation like this, and the syntax and triplet rhyme both invite us to, we can hardly dismiss the conclusion that Donne is comparing woman's love to man's and finding the former lacking, while the weight of stress on the word 'ever' emphasises this. But is it necessarily as misogynistic and condemnatory as critics have assumed? The challenge lies, as so often with Donne, and indeed any intellectually demanding poet, in grasping the whole idea, in this case the final octect in its entirety. Again the rhyme helps us to establish this division of ideas.

If we reread this final octect as a whole we should be able to see that something less troubling and more in harmony with the rest of the poem may be taking place. Donne is issuing an invitation to the girl: an invitation to become, like the angels, closer to him by adopting something less pure but still pure. By admitting him as her lover, by allowing him to make love to her, she is ennobling them both, making her own love the superior guardian of his, 'So thy love may be my loves spheare.' He is taking her, and us, way beyond conventional love poetry where each item of the girl's physical form becomes a focus for analogy and praise. So great is her worth, so profound their love, that only by making her become a heavenly sphere, containing and ruling his own, can he signify that worth. But then, just as there is a gap between the purity of angels and the purity of their air-bound form, so is there a difference between woman's and man's love, between hers and his. The difference is that *she* is the greater, the purer, the finer. The poem ends on a superb compliment. Donne is only too aware of the physical needs which drive his love and 'fixe it selfe in thy lip, eye and brow'. He allows no discussion when it comes to 'Love must not be, but take a body too', and yet the dilemma remains, does she love him? 'I saw, I had loves pinnace overfraught.' By evoking this wonderful, religious picture of their love, he hopes to win her permanently.

The poem is a conventional love poem in that it concerns itself with the age-old struggle between the frustrated male and the reluctant female. A truth Donne recognises almost with a smile in the ending: women's love is purer (if only slightly) than man's, in that it requires something more than the sexual urge to kindle it: sacrifice. The sacrifice the angels make when they adopt their ethereal form, a step down, but one with entirely holy intentions.

However we respond to these final few lines, and they entice us into responding, we should agree that *Aire and Angels* marks a considerable step up in complexity and skill from the two *Elegies*. The poem evokes something like wonder at the love it expresses and yet we will still search in vain for anything, any word or image which singles the girl out or characterises her. Donne may have worshipped every single hair on her head but we do not even know what colour it was.

So we can now remind ourselves what this first chapter has taught us in terms of analysing Donne's poetry further. The list below may seem a little daunting when looked at in isolation but it should serve from here on as an easily accessible revision tool.

1. We should read his love poetry fully aware that it was written for limited circulation amongst friends,and that Donne himself always spoke and wrote dismissively of it.
2. We need to develop an eye (and ear) for wit and the complex playing with words that is one of Donne's major characteristics.
3. Brevity of expression is often the springboard for far more complex thinking.
4. Donne is not afraid of using religious terms in poems about sexual love and had little respect for the conventions of Elizabethan love poetry.
5. Sensuality is not one of Donne's interests. What interests him is what causes him to think, not feel.
6. We should focus on sentences as units in difficult sections.
7. Even in his love poetry, the object of his love remains frustratingly anonymous.
8. The power of his religious imagery should not be underestimated.
9. We should look for divisions within the poem by rhyme or rhythm to assist our otherwise grammatical analysis.
10. Donne frequently ends a poem with a shock or major shift of some kind.

Suggested Work

Keeping these points in mind, read *Elegie* IV, *Perfume*, looking for the shift in the poem's focus from the lover he addresses to his own speculations.

- Can we distinguish clearly where this occurs?
- How distinct is Donne's treatment of the girl and the perfume?

2

Satire

A number Donne's poems are formally titled *Satyres,* although in this chapter we are not going to restrict ourselves to them. Many other poems freely employ satire and this should not surprise us given that Donne was an ambitious young man, restrained by his religion inside circles he could not quite break until he turned his back on his Catholic faith and embraced the Church of England. The poetic satire was a recognised method to draw attention to oneself. Circulated in manuscript amongst friends and potentially useful acquaintances, it was often the means to further a court career. Donne employed it in this way, and the *Satyres* themselves belong to the period of his twenties when he was at Lincoln's Inn and eager to find a place in the world. They are his earliest poems and exhibit clear signs of frustrated energy and ambition. Satire is naturally the preferred method of the young. It is easier to expose folly in others when one has had precious little time for folly of one's own. The first poem we will look at under the satire mantle is the *Song*, 'Goe, and catche a falling starre', which is quoted in full. Its relative simplicity and brevity make it easier to deal with than the formal *Satyres,* and so a more encouraging place to begin.

Song

Goe, and catche a falling starre,
Get with child a mandrake roote,
Tell me, where all past yeares are,

28

Or who cleft the Divels foot,
Teach me to heare Mermaides singing,   5
Or to keep off envies stinging,
    And finde
    What winde
Serves to advance an honest minde.

If thou beest borne to strange sights,   10
Things invisible to see,
Ride ten thousand daies and nights,
Till age snow white haires on thee,
Thou, when thou retorn'st, wilt tell mee
All strange wonders that befell thee,   15
    And sweare
    No where
Lives a woman true, and faire.

If thou findst one, let mee know,
Such a Pilgrimage were sweet;   20
Yet doe not, I would not goe,
Though at next doore wee might meet,
Though shee were true, when you met her,
And last, till you write your letter,
    Yet shee   25
    Will bee
False, ere I come, to two, or three.

A first reading may present some difficulties about vocabulary and
imagery, but the central, misogynistic thrust of the poem should be
very evident. Donne concludes that all women are duplicitous and
untrustworthy. In the time it would take for his friend's letter to
reach him, the unique object of his pilgrimage, a woman who is
both beautiful and faithful, would have been faithless, not once, but
twice or even three times. It is a bleak view, for a man.

Look now at the first verse and isolate the seven impossible tasks
Donne instructs his reader to attempt. Most should be self-explana-
tory but line 2 needs some knowledge of Elizabethan folk culture.
The mandrake was a plant people believed possessed strange proper-
ties. Most of these gave it human characteristics. It was, for example,

meant to scream when uprooted and it is frequently depicted with forked roots like legs, and had a reputation as an aphrodisiac. In this poem, Donne regards finding, or even impregnating a mandrake plant with a human child as just another absolute impossibility. And perhaps it is not too fanciful to see already (ll. 6–9), in his bitter recognition of the destructive power of envy, and the struggle for success faced by all honest men, a reflection of his own difficult situation.

The purpose of these bizarre imperatives is not explained until verse two, via an imaginary quest he makes us follow. We may be carried away to see remarkable sights, and devote our lives journeying in search of such things until old age brings us home, but when we eventually return with news of our discoveries, there is only one thing we will firmly assert. That the woman who is both beautiful and honest, faithful and admirable, is a myth.

Characteristically, having asserted this so confidently, Donne immediately undermines it by suggesting that should we find one such, we must let him know straight away so that he could meet her. 'Such a Pilgrimage were sweet;' he says, before again immediately denying it because, as initially noted, she would prove worthless even in the brief time taken by the message.

It is not difficult to see why we might regard this poem as a satire, but it might be harder to see what we might gain from doing so. Poems like *Song* frequently lead critics and readers to accuse Donne of unmitigated cynicism. Is there any way we can avoid the same, unappealing conclusion? The tone holds one route out of the dilemma. There is something gently mournful about the abrupt change of rhythm and triple rhyme which ends each verse. It is as though the poet is yearning for something better and sighing when he can't find it. This is especially pronounced in the final verse where the last line of the poem collapses completely into sad resignation:

> Yet shee
> Will bee
> False, ere I come, to two, or three.

(lines 25–7)

This is also an opportune moment to build on something we learned in our first chapter. Point four of the Chapter 1 summary suggested that Donne was never afraid to employ religious imagery in poems about sex. Now we can go even further. So completely immersed in religion and its contemporary conflicts was Donne, he can rarely write anything without religious imagery insinuating its way into the poetry. The closing lines of *Song* echo Christ's injunction to St Peter in the garden of Gethsemene. By cock crow, Christ tells Peter on the eve of the crucifixion, he will have denied knowledge of him three times, and indeed, of course, Peter does. Today, we might not even know this particular passage from the Gospel, but it would have been ingrained on Donne's heart by years of attendance at Mass and celebrating Easter. And should we doubt the possibility of this echo, I think his use of 'Pilgrimage' in line 20 only reinforces the point. For Donne, the search for a beautiful, trustworthy woman could never be merely a *quest* or a *journey*: something far more meaningful was required.

So the tone of this plaintive little lyric may redeem it from being judged unashamedly misogynistic, and the religious intensity of some of the imagery should at least reassure a female reader that Donne, even when condemning them, treats women with immense respect.

The second poem we will examine here is *Satyre 1 (On London Society)*. Read it through and try to visualise the way of life it depicts. It encourages us to go along with the satirist as he sees, and condemn what he sees. Having read it, ask yourself where does Donne focus his attack?

Initially we might answer: on his imaginary companion. Where Donne is studious, his companion is 'wild uncertaine' (l. 12). The poem opens by describing him as a 'fondling, motley humorist', and urges him to leave the poet alone with his books. Ignoring our indecorous use of the word today as a verb, 'fondling' here is an adjective built on the word 'fond' which implies foolishness. And 'motley' is a term applied to courtly fools we are perhaps familiar with from Shakespeare. Its more specific meaning relates to divergency of colour, which was the conventional dress for a fool. Both terms clearly signal Donne's superiority to his visitor whose arrival disturbs his serious reading which includes everything from 'Gods conduits, grave Divines' (l. 5) to 'Giddie fantastique Poets' (l. 10). It is a timeless situation. The young man intent on his studies, distracted by the promise of excitement on the streets by a less self-disciplined student, will always face a difficult decision – which should be something of a healthy corrective for students eager to raise the tattered flag of relevancy in literary debate.

If we now examine the way Donne describes his private rooms, we will be able to see that his grasp of the dilemma is entirely human and not mere artifice. The closet is a 'standing wooden chest,' a 'prison' and he is 'coffin'd' in it (ll. 2–4). Although he goes on to prick his companion with all the penetration of a needle-sharp pen, he recognises from the start that the temptation is real, however severely he castigates him for being weak and shallow. The books may contain great wisdom: everything from divine instruction to political acumen, but they do not prove strong enough to resist the invitation:

> Shall I leave all this constant company,
> And follow headlong, wild uncertaine thee?
>
> (ll. 11–12)

The question is almost rhetorical, although it takes another 40 lines of assurances and invective before they actually depart. However strongly we feel the narrative situation has been designed to permit the satire, we should not doubt that Donne saw the dilemma as entirely human, and if we consider what we know of his life and ambitions, we should not find this the least surprising. But this is taking us some way from the satire which permeates the poem and we can return to it by looking closely at the accusations Donne makes in the section leading up to their departure in line 52.

Before agreeing to go with him, Donne tries to gain his companion's assurance that he will not abandon him the moment he meets someone more interesting. Yet this bargain is weakened from the start by Donne's openly expressed lack of confidence.

First sweare by thy best love in earnest
(If thou which lov'st all, canst love any best)

(ll. 13–14)

Donne knows that even if he wins the assurance, it will mean little.
Although his companion's trustworthiness is under attack, beyond
this we need to consider precisely what the target of the satire is. If
we reread lines 13–26 we can form an opinion. Taking the three
types, soldier, courtier, judge, which Donne uses to illustrate his
companion's tendency to wander, we should note that what they
offer the companion is really the same thing, preferment. In the case
of the 'Captaine' and 'Justice' that gain is even more obviously
equated with money. The 'Captaine' is

Bright parcell gilt, with forty dead mens pay,

(l. 18)

and the 'Justice', with his train of officers, has a 'beautious sonne
and heire!' to offer. The courtier's wealth is indicated by the gaudy
adjectives, 'briske perfum'd piert', the latter an alternative spelling of
'pert' which carried much more negative weight for Donne's age
than for ours where it often implied a boldness and audacity which
was inappropriate. The word carries none of the connotations of
'cuteness' it has today. All three of these figures, Donne imagines,
would prove instantly more attractive company than himself
because his companion is seeking something Donne is not: material
or social gain. In a witty parody of the marriage vows, Donne
demands that his friend eschew all such temptations and remain
with him:

For better or for worse take mee, or leave mee:
To take, and leave me is adultery.

(ll. 25–6)

It has become a moral issue. What Donne decries is not just the self-
ishness, but the lack of morality. In this first section he has created a
picture of a society bloated with its own success and motivated by
greed. This accusation becomes clearer in the lines that follow, where

Donne savages his friend's behaviour so successfully he finally proves contrite in lines 49–52.

If we examine the section from line 27 to line 48, we can see this picture develop. He chastises his friend for being hypocritical:

> Oh monstrous, superstitious puritan,
> Of refin'd manners, yet ceremoniall man,
>
> (ll. 27–8)

for being puritanical in his readiness to condemn others, yet wholly enslaved to the petty rituals of social practice. Donne describes his friend responding to each new encounter 'like a needy broker', gauging the value of the individual by his dress and outward appearance and exhibiting courtesy accordingly. He is incapable of kindness, 'That wilt comfort none', unless he sees the chance for personal gain by inheriting their property or property they themselves hope to inherit:

> What lands hee hath in hope, or of his owne,
>
> (l. 34)

The logical conclusion of this attitude has the friend's 'companions' all formally leaving their property to him, mimicking the property rights of marriage. Not only does Donne build on the previous accusation about adultery here, he also turns the criticism into another opportunity for wit where 'deare' is a pun, intimate and expensive.

Having clearly put his companion's failings on public display, Donne takes a bold step and asks the central question of the whole satire. If we omit his parenthesis we can see it very easily:

> Why should'st thou . . .
> Hate vertue, though shee be naked, and bare?
>
> (ll. 37–41)

He sets up a strident antithesis, with virtue on one side and his companion (and all he represents) on the other. We can see from this why satirists are considered dangerous and why Donne gave up the habit when he had found patronage amongst the nobility. In a letter to Henry Wootton he requested him not to copy his work or allow it to be seen widely since, 'to my satires there belongs some fear, and to some elegies,. . .I am desirous to hide them.'[1]

The parenthesis itself again shows his friend to be a hypocrite since he not only approves of nakedness in his 'plumpe muddy whore, or prostitute boy' but indeed relishes it, in the wonderfully acerbic phrase, 'ranke itchie lust'. Donne's next step employs imagery we should feel familiar with. At birth and death we are naked, but until the moment our souls become naked, 'unapparrelled /Of bodies,' they can not attain heaven. Nakedness is in fact a 'blest state' which was undone by Adam and Eve's orginal sin. Donne himself is now clothed merely in 'coarse attire' but nonetheless is able to communicate 'With God, and with the Muses', we presume by his reading and by prayer. What necessity is there, Donne implies, for anything richer or better; for the gaudiness and excess of the court? At this point the unfortunate companion appears to acknowledge the truth of Donne's words and become 'a contrite penitent,' who 'dost repent./ These vanities, and giddinesses,' sufficiently for Donne to leave his sombre closet for the bustle of the streets, in his company.

We can now make use of a tactic employed in Chapter 1 to explore the next short section of the poem from lines 53 to 64. It has been suggested that the lengthy sentences and complex syntax Donne sometimes employs make it difficult for the modern reader used to far briefer, less intense usages of English. We pointed out that it was an advantage to read a sentence as a whole, and try and grasp its meaning intact if possible. Even though we might not be able to do this initially, we can often grasp its structure; if it is a list, for example, or an answered question, or a digression, and this takes us one step further towards complete understanding. Do this now; and to make it easier, the sentence in question is reproduced below. Reread it, carefully and consciously using the punctuation as a guide to treat it as one sentence:

> But sooner may a cheape whore, who hath beene
> Worne by as many severall men in sinne,
> As are black feathers, or musk-colour hose,

> Name her childs right true father, 'mongst all those:
> Sonner may one guesse, who shall beare away
> The Infanta of London, Heire to an India;
> And sooner may a gulling weather Spie
> By drawing forth heavens Scheme tell certainly
> What fashioned hats, or ruffes, or suits next yeare
> Our subtile-witted antique youths will weare;
> Than thou, when thou depart'st from mee, canst show
> Whither, why, when, or with whom thou wouldst go.
>
> (ll. 53–64)

We should be able to see it is really three examples followed by a conclusion, each example being introduced by the same 'sooner may' phrase, and a conclusion beginning, 'Than thou' (l. 63). It makes sense to examine each example in turn, and because they rely on contemporary social practice they might still resist understanding without help. In the first example we have a whore, so experienced, she has been employed as often as people wear black feathers or musk-coloured (reddish brown) tights to hide the fact they they are dirty. The wit depends on the usage of 'Worne' to apply to the clothes and to her use by men, and of course there is the extra sense of something being worn out, which adds to the superior moral tone adopted throughout the poem. Such a whore, Donne asserts, is as likely to know the true father of her child amongst all her customers (l. 56) as . . . and we can either then wait for the rest of the comparison, or jump straight to line 63 for it.

The second example concerns some unspecified rich London heiress, and which is likely, amongst all the numerous and eager candidates, to win her as his bride. 'India' is used typically by Donne because of its excess. Looking for a way of making her sound incredibly wealthy, Donne finds the most exotic and richest comparison he can, the East. For his final example of impossible guesses, Donne uses 'a gulling weather Spie', a charlatan who studies the weather to tell the future; in this case, what type of clothes fashionable young men will be wearing next year. A 'ruffe' is an elaborate lace collar familiar in the portraiture of the period, and the spelling of 'antique' for our 'antic' may also have been a minor hurdle.

Finally, in lines 63–4, Donne provides us with the remaining half of the comparison. Once on the street, his companion is so spoilt for choice, so excited by the prospect before him, so incapable of decision, he is every bit as impossible to govern as the whore, the Infanta or the Spie.

As confirmation, and to encourage the practice of analysing difficult passages this way, below is the same passage with each of the main subjects and their corresponding verbs in bold type. The connections are far easier to see. In line 57 the subject *one*, and verb *guess*, are adjacent:

> But sooner may **a cheape whore**, who hath beene
> Worne by as many severall men in sinne
> As are black feathers, or musk-colour hose,
> **Name** her childs right true father, 'mongst all those:
> Sooner may **one guesse**, who shall beare away
> The Infanta of London, Heire to an India;
> And sooner may **a gulling weather Spie**
> By drawing forth heavens Scheme **tell** certainly
> What fashioned hats, or ruffes, or suits next yeare
> Our subtile-witted antique youths will weare;
> Than **thou**, when thou depart'st from mee, canst **show**
> Whither, why, when, or with whom thou **wouldst go**.
>
> (ll. 53–64)

Throughout the poem Donne characterises fashionable young men as shallow, foolish, arrogant, and so apparently intent on humour they are incapable of seeing their own folly – which makes them perfect targets for satire.

'Now we are in the street' Donne says and the present tense takes us into the confusion with him. Addressing his companion as 'He' (l. 67), furthers our complicity with the poet and encourages us to enjoy the satire. Again we have a lengthy sentence, but one which is less difficult because it is mostly descriptive and only uses an analogy towards the end, where the companion's impatience is compared to apprentices or schoolboys who are trapped in their place of work, knowing there is some exciting activity they are missing outside:

As prentises, or schoole-boyes which doe know
Of some gay sport abroad, yet dare not goe.

(ll. 75–6)

Before that we see Donne's friend 'hem'd in' by Donne against the street wall, prevented from greeting 'Every fine silken painted foole we meet,' yet itching to ingratiate himself with them all. And as a violinist has to stop the string at the lowest position on the finger-board to reach the highest note, so his friend bends lowest to the grandest people they meet. '[M]ost brave' (l. 78) does not imply physical or moral courage here, but something more akin to brash-ness or showiness. We then have two very specific references to deal with. Though moved to extreme displays of courtesy by the 'most brave', his friend seems incapable of even noticing those Donne regards with some respect. To emphasise this Donne compares him to a performing horse, immobile unless instructed to move, and to elephants and apes which would respond to the King of Spain's name with the same incomprehension as any other. At a time when explorers were just beginning to return from America and the East, not only with tales of strange beasts and sights, but with the real things, exhibitions of exotic animals (and peoples) were very popular in Elizabethan London.

We are again encouraged to see with Donne's eyes as his friend 'leaps' with excitement on spotting a young man apparently renowned for his dancing. The use of dialogue here, and elsewhere in the poem, reinforces our sense of immediacy and complicity with the poet. It is as though Donne is speaking directly to us, an invis-ible third, as he walks along with his frantic companion. Reprimanded by Donne for dancing around himself, the companion is subdued a little before they meet a man smoking so heavily, Donne condemns him too with, ''T may be you smell him not, truely I doe' although the words fall on deaf ears, other than ours. His companion, spying a particularly well-dressed young man, manages to leave Donne for a moment to speak to the 'many-coloured Peacock' but returns merely to praise him as the finest courtier in matters of dress, as though merely knowing him will somehow impress Donne (and us). Dismissing the well-dressed courtier as food for comedians, Donne is this time himself reprimanded as his friend assures him that the courtier is well travelled and speaks fluent French and Italian. The subtlety of the poet–reader relationship is considerable here, as Donne interjects his own aside (l. 102) in parenthesis, to point out that his companion speaks neither language. Donne seems to be assuming we have followed him so closely in this journey, imagined and satirical, that we are absolutely of his mind when he finally turns on his companion with the rebuke, 'So is the Poxe'; which not only reminds us of the moral superiority he has claimed all along, but of our own mortality. The pox was a loose term for all venereal diseases, but especially syphilis which was a disfiguring and fatal disease in Donne's age. It was also frequently referred to as the French or Spanish disease.

At this, the companion is both silenced and alienated, seeking out 'More men of sort, of parts, and qualities' until he at last encounters his lover in a window, the final signal to depart from Donne, who has all along been merely a convenience, and is accordingly 'like light dew exhal'd':

> At last his Love he in a windowe spies,
> And like light dew exhal'd, he flings from mee
> Violently ravish'd to his lechery.
>
> (ll. 106–8)

But Donne has the final word, and in the last few lines projects events forward to the aftermath in which his companion ends up crawling back to him, his head bowed in shame, and takes to his bed to recover.

A review of the sections of the poem we have discussed above will help us to understand how Donne's poems often proceed like logical, or pseudo-logical arguments, moving from one point to the next in a deliberate manner towards a conclusion.

The first section, lines 1–26, depicts Donne in his study resisting his companion's call to leave his books and join him in the street. It concludes with Donne attempting to gain an assurance from the friend that he will not abandon him at the first sign of more attractive company.

The second section, lines 27–52, sees Donne castigating the companion for his immorality and hypocrisy through a description of his normal behaviour. None the less, it ends with Donne giving in to the request because his friend appears appropriately contrite.

The third section, lines 53–64, is a self-mocking recognition of Donne's stupidity in giving in, since the companion immediately shows no sign of either purpose or calm. Donne is left stunned by his friend's childish excitability.

The fourth section, lines 65–108, is a description of their walk in the street, including proof of all the weaknesses the companion has been accused of, until the companion finally deserts Donne and heads off in pursuit of his own pleasure.

The final section, lines 109–12, is a brief account of the aftermath, as the errant companion returns to Donne, head bowed in shame, suitably ashamed of his rashly selfish, immoral behaviour.

Now we can take stock and consider *Satyre* I as a whole. Initially we accepted that the focus of the satire was Donne's impossibly superficial companion. But now we can be even more specific. The little trip he takes us on exhibits all sorts of poor behaviour, but it is poor because underneath it stems from the same impulses, material greed and lust. The various targets Donne shoots down in this savage and energetic attack, are all intent on selfish pursuits, whether courtly self-advancement or mere sexual gratification. It is an undilutedly Christian, if not Catholic, stance, and at its heart is the court. As a young man Donne invested enormous energy trying to gain a prominent position in the court and finally, under James I, succeeded, but his early years were spent floundering, hampered first by his religion and then by his secretive, ill-judged marriage to Anne More.

The Legacie is the third poem we will analyse in this chapter. It appears complete below. Read it through and consider why it might find its way into a chapter on satire.

The Legacie

When I dyed last, and, Deare, I dye
   As often as from thee I goe,
   Though it be but an houre agoe,
And Lovers houres be full eternity,
I can remember yet, that I   5
   Something did say, and something did bestow;
Though I be dead, which sent mee, I should be
Mine owne executor and Legacie.

I heard mee say, Tell her anon,
   That my selfe, (that is you, not I,)   10
   Did kill me, and when I felt mee dye,
I bid mee send my heart, when I was gone,
But I alas could there finde none,
   When I had ripp'd me, 'and search'd where hearts did lye;   15
It kill'd mee againe, that I who still was true,
In life, in my last Will should cozen you.

Yet I found something like a heart,
   But colours it, and corners had,
   It was not good, it was not bad,   20
It was intire to none, and few had part.
As good as could be made by art
   It seem'd; and therefore for our losses sad,
I meant to send this heart in stead of mine,
But oh, no man could hold it, for twas thine.   25

Although we may have only a cursory understanding of the poem after one reading, since it is maddeningly obtuse, provided we have appreciated a little of the irony of the final couplet, we ought to recognise it contains a sentiment similar to the *Song* which we analysed at the start of this chapter. Donne dismisses his lover as faithless, possessing a heart incapable of loving only one man. But this is a brutally superficial comment of what is an edgily witty conclusion to a beautiful example of Elizabethan love poetry. *The Legacie* is a model poem of Donne's, and much of what we discover in this analysis can be applied to many of his poems. It combines scintillating wit and ingenuity with a beauty of form, none of which detracts one iota from the essential human feeling conveyed between the lovers.

The startling wit is evident from the first line with his assertion that dying is something he does all the time, 'When I dyed last.' How far we wish to read sexual allusion into the use of 'dying' is perhaps up to us, but Donne is certainly more interested in using it to permit his toying with the idea of leaving a will, of being both executor and legacy. He then reminds his lover that every departure from her is a kind of death, even though he left her only a hour before, as everyone knows, 'Lovers houres be full eternity.' The latter half of the first verse imagines him leaving behind something of himself, yet spoken by him too, 'Something did say, and something did bestow' which allows him the dual function of executor and legacy. In the second verse, the deliberate toying with words becomes so self-conscious that he feels the need to actually qualify for his lover who is speaking of what, '(that is you, not I,)'. Donne knows what he is suggesting is complex and convoluted. Part of the poem's technique is to goad the lover into paying attention by drawing attention to its difficulty. We can see this if we examine the lines concerned closely. What at first might just appear confusing becomes something deliberate and designed:

> I heard mee say, Tell her anon,
> That my selfe, (that is you, not I,)
>
> (ll. 9–10)

How can 'my selfe' become 'you'? The two terms are logically opposed. Donne is raising the conventional notion of lovers' unity which he is so fond of exploring. Repeatedly he finds different ways to describe that feeling of newness, and yet loss of individual identity, which lovers commonly experience. In love, you become a different person, a new creature with one identity, and the simple, colloquial language he employs here suggests he knows his lover knows it too. It is something so obvious he can refer to it as a teacher reminding a pupil of a previously learned fact.

In this verse, the lover, presumably by her neglect, kills Donne, who as he dies bequeaths her his heart. Here the puzzle intensifies. Imagining his own chest 'ripp'd' open, he searches vainly inside for the heart which ought naturally to be there. Finding none, he has yet another means to chastise the lover but still declare the strength of his love:

> It kill'd mee againe, that I who still was true,
> In life, in my last Will should cozen you.'

(ll. 16–17)

Having been killed once by her, he dies a second time when he realises that his dying wish (to leave her his heart) cannot be fulfilled and he must 'cozen' her. Commonly in use during Donne's age, the word 'cozen' means to dupe or deceive and has a rough modern equivalent in 'con'. However poorly treated he might imagine he has been, he still asserts that he loves her, which of course only aims to fuel the lover's guilt.

In the third verse Donne finds 'something like a heart,' and his description of it might strike us initially as curious. It should do. It has 'colours' and 'corners', was neither 'good' nor 'bad', and while few had a part in it, it gave itself to no one in particular. Careful to avoid too much offence and therefore undermine his attempt to recapture her, Donne makes her heart morally neutral but cleverly points out that it is neither promiscuous nor untried. We should also not underestimate the terms 'colours' and 'corners'. Both carry considerable weight within Donne's work as a whole and, as John Carey argues, Donne was fascinated by anything which involved the meeting of opposites, corners: hence his love of paradox.[2]

This strange heart is almost believable, almost convincing, 'As good as could be made by art', where 'art' really means any creative act, not simply painting as we might be tempted to think today. So Donne decides to send this one 'for our losses sad', as his legacy. As so often with Donne, the poem's true sting is left for the final moment and here he triumphs as he asserts the impossibility of sending this heart, because 'no man could hold it, for twas thine'. The witty idea that her heart is so slippery, no one can physically grasp it, and therefore by analogy she is impossible to love and incapable of loving, is a magnificent poetic coup. Saved as it is for the final line, after so much deliberate confusion and complexity, the idea's simplicity carries greater momentum, and it would be a dull lover indeed who would not feel the weight of it.

We are now in a position to summarise what we have learned from this chapter to add to the points in Chapter 1.

1. A lot of Donne's early poetry is energetically and consciously satirical.
2. Donne is capable of confidently asserting something and immediately denying it.
3. Analysis of a poem's rhythm will help lead us to a fuller understanding of its tone.
4. Donne's subject-matter may initially appear rooted in his era but is often timeless.
5. Donne's satire is often deeply moral at its heart.
6. We can analyse the longer sentences by carefully locating and highlighting the key subjects and their verbs.
7. Donne consciously tries to make the reader complicit in a satirical attack.
8. Donne's violent hatred of the court is understandable by remembering he was both an ex-Catholic and an outsider.
9. Donne is equally at ease using colloquial language, as he is using elaborate poetic imagery when the poem requires him to.
10. We should always be alert to the use of paradox in Donne.

Suggested Work

• Read *Satyre* II *(On Lawyers)*. Then analyse in detail ll. 21–38:

> And they who write to Lords, rewards to get,. . .
> In which Commandements large receipt they dwell.

by locating the key subjects and their verbs and then highlighting them.

• Read *Satyre* IIII (*On the Court*) and analyse ll. 155–68:

> At home in wholesome solitarinesse . . .
> Such as swells the bladder of our court?

in the same way.

3

The Intensity of Love

A cursory glance through Donne's *Songs and Sonnets* would convince most novices that Donne is a love poet. Poem after poem dives in with the word and several use it openly in the title.: *Loves Usury, Lovers Infinitenesse, Loves Growth, Loves Alchemie, Loves Deitie.* Yet, as we have already discovered, Donne is no Petrarch or Dante, persistently adoring a Laura or a Beatrice. The experience of love fascinates him, and stimulates him to engage with it in a variety of forms. The conventional eulogy, the poem which sets out to adore or worship the woman by praising her, is one Donne rarely attempts. And as we have seen in *Elegie* XIX, *To his Mistris going to Bed,* even when he does so, he is incapable of settling for mere physical beauty, and we end up no wiser about her looks or character than we began.

It is the experience itself and its maddening ambiguities which drive Donne to write about it so frequently. Physical gratification, the consummation of a courtship, may often be placed at a poem's heart, but taken as a whole, the *Songs and Sonnets* are more concerned with what love does to the mind than to the body. What he explores is what takes place inside his own head, and if what happens there is worth sharing with his lover, then Donne is always eager to try and give those thoughts poetic form. In this chapter we will be looking specifically at poems where the experience of love is self-consciously the central issue. This will enable us to consider a number of related questions. How far does Donne detail the experience or merely reflect on it? How and for what reasons does he employ eulogy? Does he ever seek to sound autobiographical? And, ultimately, can his meditations on love communicate effectively with us today?

We'll begin with an analysis of *The Good-Morrow*, a poem which has justifiably found its way into numerous anthologies over the years. It is quoted here in full.

The Good-Morrow

I wonder by my troth, what thou, and I
Did, till we lov'd? were we not wean'd till then?
But suck'd on countrey pleasures, childishly?
Or snorted we in the seaven sleepers den?
T'was so; But this, all pleasures fancies bee.   5
If ever any beauty I did see,
Which I desir'd, and got, t'was but a dreame of thee.

And now good morrow to our waking soules,
Which watch not one another out of feare;
For love, all love of other sights controules,   10
And makes one little roome, and every where.
Let sea-discoverers to new worlds have gone,
Let Maps to other, worlds on worlds have showne,
Let us possesse one world, each hath one, and is one.

My face in thine eye, thine in mine appeares,   15
And true plaine hearts doe in the faces rest,
Where can we finde two better hemispheares
Without sharpe North, without declining West?
What ever dyes, was not mixt equally;
If our two loves be one, or, thou and I   20
Love so alike, that none doe slacken, none can die.

To some extent this poem is highly conventional. It takes place at dawn, after a night making love, and as such can be described as an *aubade*. The term can be used of poetry or music, but in either case is always associated with the drowsy bliss of a post-coital dawn. Romeo and Juliet's shared ornithological ignorance about larks and nightingales is perhaps the most likely place readers have encountered the aubade before. Unlike Shakespeare, who has a dramatic obligation (and no lighting), Donne does not make it clear this is an aubade until verse two, 'And now good morrow to our waking soules,' and even then we are not sure quite whether these are 'soules' or bodies waking. The image which begins verse three, of his seeing his own reflection in his lover's eyes, provides the confirmation we needed. Here are two lovers, so physically close that they can see each other's reflections clearly in their eyes.

We will begin by considering the list of rhetorical questions Donne asks in verse one. What, he asks, did we do before we fell in love? Were we such infants? 'not wean'd till then?' And continuing the breast-feeding image, he enforces the idea of their previous experiences as childish by calling them 'countrey pleasures', unsophisticated, raising the possibility of an indecent pun on 'countrey' which would also heighten the quality of this new love. The seven sleepers of line 4 refers to the myth of seven Christian youths who escaped Roman persecution by sleeping in a cave for centuries. All these combine to create a sensation familiar to lovers: the notion that whatever has taken place before was in some fundamental way only fragmentary, unfulfilled, substantially impoverished in some essentially human way we find difficult to quantify. Donne opts for childishness as his central metaphor until the final three lines of the verse where a triple rhyme reinforces a new point. 'But this, all pleasures fancies bee', he exclaims. This love is the only reality, everything else is imagination. Beautiful women he had formerly desired, and enjoyed, now become mere dreams compared to the girl in this bed. It is a potent compliment if we dwell on it for a moment. In the context of love poetry, dreams are usually indicative of joy and ecstasy. We talk of 'the girl of our dreams' and 'I must be dreaming' when the pleasures are so intense they seem to outstrip reality. Here, the girl in Donne's bed becomes so superb that the realities of his experience of love with other beautiful women are turned into dreams of her. Hyperbole is an instinctive gift in Donne. Think of a way of exaggerating something and he will inevitably take it one step further.

At this point we can consider the form of address the poem adopts. There is no dialogue, no direct speech. Yet the girl's presence is not in question. The frequent use of personal pronouns and emphasis on joint experience make this clearly a love poem in its *need* to communicate. Although we may eventually conclude that it deals with what happens in the poet's mind, it doesn't take place in some semi-conscious, post-orgasmic trance. The girl is there, it is morning and they are both extremely conscious and aware of what has taken place. What Donne gives us is a recreation of a stage in their developing love, the moment when *he* realises how significant this event is and conveys that realisation to his lover. It really is a new dawn, a 'good-morrow'.

Close on the affirmation of this new dawn at the start of verse two come strengthening claims. Their souls are watchful, not out of fear but because love now controls all they see. They love to see only that which love dictates they see. 'For love, all love of other sights controules'. Added to this is a toying with concepts of space which Donne enjoys applying to lovers, and which we will encounter repeatedly in the *Songs and Sonnets*. So all-encompassing is the sensation, so quenching the feeling of completeness that comes with being in love, that the smallest room serves as a universe. Donne leaves the travelling, the exploring, to others. He has his kingdom, his entire world, here in the confines of this bed. 'Let us possesse one world, each hath one, and is one.' It may be helpful here to try and understand this sequence of images in verse two with a clear sense of Elizabethan geography. In an age of fragile wooden vessels taking years to return (if they ever did) from astoundingly risky voyages, the noun 'world' had a very different grip on the imagination.

The final verse of the poem begins with the observation already touched on of the lovers being able to see each other reflected in their eyes. In itself it is a dramatic way of demonstrating what he has already affirmed, that in some mysterious way they have exchanged being, souls. Using the commonplace that the face is a voice to the heart, he proudly proclaims their superiority and unity as two halves of one sphere:

Where can we finde two better hemispheares
Without sharpe North, without declining West?

(ll. 17–18)

The addition of the negative adjectives to the points of the compass, ('sharpe' for cold and 'declining' for the sunset) appears to be an almost humorous assertion that the lovers have only positive qualities.

The final three lines of the poem are undoubtedly difficult, and 'Dyes' is to be found spelled both ways in differing editions. Although initially this might strike a new student of Donne as a serious issue, it really doesn't present any difficulty. The distinction between the spellings is a fairly modern one. The ambiguity is really what matters here. A modern reader would probably initially read a meaning that hints at colouring something by mixing unequal amounts, and see this as a metaphorical comment on the perfect balance of their love, and then, by implication, its immortality. However, a more likely reading for Donne's contemporaries would have been one which recognised the idea that only impure things are mortal – a reading which impels the poem on to its concluding thought more comfortably. If, he suggests, they love so equally, so perfectly, that each love is indistinguishable from the other, or that they love each other with unfailing constancy, 'none doe slacken', then they will achieve immortality, 'none can die'. None is of course a pronoun contracted from 'no one' and if we think of it as such in that final line, some of the difficulty may dissipate. Perhaps most importantly what we must take from them is the grand assertion of the magnificence of their love, its immense potential, even to the point of immortality.

An interesting game to play with Donne's love poetry is to try and place yourself in the imaginary recipient's position. How would a woman feel, respond, if presented with such a poem? What might she think? Frequently, although Donne is not employing the obvious eulogy of more conventional love poetry, he is devastatingly more complimentary. He engages his lover on the highest intellectual plane: and assumes she is capable of joining him there. George Puttenham in his *The Arte of English Poesie* (1598), describing how important a part poetry played in the courtship etiquette of the time, advises using it, 'sometimes honouring, auancing, praising: an other while railing, reuiling, and cursing: then sorrowing, weeping, lamenting: in the end laughing, reioysing and solacing the beloued againe, with a thousand delicate deuises, odes, songs, elegies, ballads, sonets and other ditties, moouing one way and another to great compassion'.[1]

In these terms, *Loves Usury* is a bold and youthful poem, full of confidence and vitality, and at first reading we might feel it is openly immoral in its declaration of sexual independence. It is reproduced complete.

Loves Usury

For every houre that thou wilt spare mee now,
    I will allow,
Usurious God of Love, twenty to thee,
When with my browne, my gray haires equall bee;
Till then, Love, let my body raigne, and let   5
Mee travell, sojourne, snatch, plot, have, forget,
Resume my last yeares relict: thinke that yet
    We'had never met.

Let mee thinke any rivalls letter mine,
    And at next nine   10
Keepe midnights promise; mistake by the way
The maid, and tell the Lady of that delay;
Onely let mee love none, no, but the sport;
From country grasse, to comfitures of Court,
Or cities quelque choses, let report   15
    My mind transport.

This bargaine's good; if when I'am old, I bee
    Inflam'd by thee,
If thine owne honour, or my shame, or paine,
Thou covet most, at that age thou shalt gaine.   20
Doe thy will then, then subject and degree,
And fruit of love, Love I submit to thee,
Spare mee till then, I'll beare it, though she bee
    One that loves mee.

Usury, or the lending of money at interest, was a sin until some time in the twelfth century. In *The Merchant of Venice* Shylock is castigated by Antonio because he is a usurer and at one point in the play Shylock retaliates and lectures Antonio, citing an Old Testament story as justification for his way of doing business. In Donne's day a usurer was not a sympathetic figure by any means, and the poem's title recognises that Love is an exacting master.

Nonetheless, the youthful Donne launches into the poem with a Faustian eagerness, willingly giving up 20 hours of his middle age for every one in love he enjoys now. 'Till then, Love, let my body raigne,' clearly declares that the poet is thinking about sexual love. The nefarious intrigues of the courtly lover are then listed in a way which seems almost lip-smacking in its rhythm, ending with the negative force of 'forget' to assure us that this is all about numbers. The verse finishes with Donne picking up his lover of the previous year 'last yeares relict' as though she were an entirely new experience: hardly respectful of the girl and quite a shift of thinking if we still have *The Good-Morrow* in mind.

The exact nature of the amorous encounter that forms the first half of verse two has exercised a number of critics who argue over whether the letter involved is from the lady to the rival, or the rival to the lady, or a whole bundle of other permutations. The innocent looking word 'any' can help us resolve this problem quite easily, because if Donne is thinking in terms of having numerous rivals and numerous ladies, which sounds fair in view of verse one, then all he is envisaging is being in a position to intercept his rivals' letters and beat them to the rendezvous. And if that were not a tart enough pleasure for him, he imagines himself bumping into the maid *en route* and not only enjoying her too, but telling the lady concerned that was why he was delayed. It all adds up to a riotously liberal picture, precisely the kind of sexual fantasy which has excited every generation of young men since Adam. Appreciating it as such, he then goes on to the central issue of the poem. 'Onely let mee love none, no, but the sport', he declares. Sex itself becomes an end in itself, love being denied and ignored completely. The verse then ends with Donne transported by talk of exciting women, from whatever social class or root, 'country grasse' to 'cities quelque choses', the latter French expression meaning 'fancy dishes' or 'sweetmeats'.

It is only in the third verse that we approach the kind of deeper thinking which we have been meeting elsewhere, thinking which counters the frequently adopted stance that this has to be a poem from Donne's youth. It may well be, but the closing thoughts are not as youthful as the rest of the poem might lead us to expect. Donne is convinced of the value of his bargain with the God of Love but for an odd reason:

> This bargaine's good; if when I'am old, I bee
>   Inflam'd by thee,'
>
> (ll. 16–17)

Why, we might ask, would he want to be driven to passionate extremes in old age? The subsequent lines delay our understanding and contain an enticement to Love. Donne is confident that Love not only has most to gain in terms of honour should he fall in love in old age, but the additional pleasure (and he is after all a usurious God) of enjoying Donne's 'shame, or paine'. Submitting himself to Love and his bargain, he readily places all aspects of that future love in Love's hands. The person, the extremity or quality, even the children, 'fruit of love', Donne will allow the God of Love to control, if he is spared the experience until then. But the poem retains its most potent and provocative thought for the end:

> Spare mee till then, I'll beare it, though she bee
>   One that loves mee.
>
> (ll. 23–4)

Why is it provocative? What is so surprising about this last condition? The commonest reading of these lines has the poem end on a note of high cynicism, a reading which merely adds the cream topping to the braggart masculinity that he has whipped up so cleverly and equitably. Let me alone until then, Donne appears to say, and I will suffer it even if she turns out to be a woman who is actually in love with me! This is breathtakingly cynical, so unmitigating it is almost inhuman, and that severity, that unworried, blinkered thinking should make us question further.

If we go back and look at *Song* we will find these lines in the final verse where Donne is asking his friend to let him know if he finds a woman who is both faithful and beautiful:

> Though at next door we might meet;
> Though she were true, when you met her,
> And last, till you write your letter,
>   Yet she
>   Will be
> False, ere I come, to two, or three.
>
> (*Song* ll. 22–7)

It is the use of 'Though' we need to study. Here Donne uses it as a contraction of 'although', and if we have the same usage in *Loves Usury* a very different, far more satisfying meaning can be read into the ending. After all the apparently youthful confidence, the delight in pursuing sexual pleasure free from all emotional involvement, we find Donne suddenly turning the whole tone of the poem on its head. He will make this bargain with the usurious God of Love granting that, or supposing that the woman Love chooses is one who loves him. What he actually values and appreciates is that very love, a rare prize worth enjoying in his old age *because* so elusive in his youth. And one final piece of evidence to offer in support of this reading: it is unusual to find a poem by Donne which ends mundanely; far more common are endings which shock or challenge our thinking, frequently with a brilliance difficult to find elsewhere in English poetry.

Something along these lines occurs at the end of the next poem to be discussed in this chapter, *The Flea*. It is often the poem students of Donne encounter first, perhaps because it has an audacity which many teachers recognise as valuable bait. Read it and then take a few minutes to reflect on what it might add to our growing appreciation of Donne's love poetry, perhaps writing a few notes to help you clarify your ideas, before continuing with the analysis here.

However squeamishly we react to the image of a flea feeding off the two lovers in the poem, we should not let it affect our understanding. Not only was the real situation a commonplace for any Renaissance man or woman, whatever their social class, it was also a favourite motif in love poetry and has a long history, especially in erotic or satirical verse. There is even a collection of such poems, *La Puce de Madame des Roches*, dated 1582, which includes poems in French, Spanish, Italian, Latin and Greek. If we are tempted at first to see the poem as ingenious and amusing because of its central action, we must resist this too and realise that what Donne is actually doing is playing with a conventional theme in a bold and original manner. The conventional poems usually revolve around the male poet imagining himself the flea and include all the predictable jokes about freedom of access, as well as appetite, on untouched female flesh. Not surprisingly, Donne is way ahead of them.

The poem opens with a direct address. Donne is lecturing his lover and takes only two lines to let us know he is engaged in the age-old struggle every heterosexual young man will recognise. He wants to have sex with her: she isn't interested. As the wily Cressida appreciates in Shakespeare's *Troilus and Cressida*:

> Things won are done, joy's soul lies in the doing.
> That she beloved knows nought that knows not this:
> Men prize the thing ungained more than it is.
> (*Troilus and Cressida*, I. ii. ll. 299–301)

Donne's mistress is every bit as determined and in control as Cressida. She is so entirely unimpressed by the arguments he makes in the first verse, that the second verse starts with her about to kill the licentious flea for taking such unwonted liberties with her. Those arguments should not be too difficult to follow. Firstly, Donne attempts to imply that the act he wishes her to indulge in is something essentially trivial, as insignificant as the flea itself, 'How little that which thou deny'st me is'. The flea having sucked his blood and then hers, he takes a far bolder step and suggests that because their blood is now mixed in the flea's body, they are in some meaningful physical way joined already, 'And in this flea, our two bloods mingled bee.' Note the girl has not been given any opportunity yet to argue. Donne is carried away with his own audacity and gallops on to the next step, which is an ingenious extension of his original assertion. Not only is copulation a thing as slight as a flea, it brings with it no shame or moral dimension at all:

> Thou know'st this cannot be said
> A sinne, nor shame, nor losse of maidenhead,
>
> (ll. 5–6)

Worse still, the flea is able to satisfy itself 'before it wooe,' and appears to be swollen as much with pleasure as with their blood, 'And pamper'd swells with one blood made of two'. How we react to the final line of the verse may well depend on our gender. Is Donne whining? Is he coaxing her in an amusing way? Whatever our response here, the girl's is not in question. As already noted, she says nothing but threatens to kill the flea and has to be prevented by Donne, who raises the tempo of his appeal and the quality of his argument.

The flea has a stay of execution as Donne tells the girl she is about to kill three lives, hers, his and the flea's. It is a remarkable leap from insignificance to mass murder but Donne takes it with alacrity, not even hesitating before turning the flea into a symbol, not of their love, but of their marriage. The rhythm of the verse appears to mimic the game being played out as Donne is brought to a full stop at the end of line 11 by his own cheek. We can almost imagine the girl's eyes opening wider as she calmly and silently demands an explanation. Donne is of course more than equal to the challenge and explains that the flea *is* both of them, and has even become a religious symbol of their unity in spite of her reluctance and parents. This stage of the debate is brought to a marked climax with the kind of wit and inventiveness which is characteristic of Donne at his best:

> Though parents grudge, and you, w'are met,
> And cloysterd in these living walls of Jet.
>
> (ll. 14–15)

The word 'cloysterd' brings monastic piety to the event and the metaphorical use of 'Jet', a glossy black stone, to describe the flea's hard, shiny carapace is stunningly original and apt.

Once more rhythm aids our appreciation of the dramatic situation and, as the forceful break formed by 'Jet' appears not to have brought results, Donne has to find a new reason to save the flea in the final three lines of the verse. Adopting again the wounded tone of the frustrated male, he quickly reminds her that although she may well be used to hurting him, 'Though use make you apt to kill mee', she should at least save herself and by so doing avoid the sacrilege of suicide, which all adds up to three sins.

It is all to no avail, and verse three opens with Donne's outraged response 'Cruell and sodaine' to her squashing the unfortunate flea against her fingernail. Claiming the flea was wholly innocent, except in that it bit her, he fakes shock at her obvious delight:

> Yet thou triumph'st, and saist that thou
> Find'st not thy self, nor mee the weaker now;
>
> (ll. 23–4)

We may also pause here to appreciate that Donne has never given the girl a voice. That she speaks to him is obvious from his responses, but that he chooses not to give her words is interesting. Instead he reports her triumph, and by making it contain a marked and deliberate counter argument, (the flea's death has not weakened either of them) he sets her up for the final lash of the velvet scourge he has been wielding all along. Again using a triple rhyme to contain the idea, he turns her rebuke against her with breathtaking deftness and confidence. Wielding a paradox to wrong-foot her, "Tis true, then learne how false', Donne revels in the idea that the girl's giving him her virginity will be as insignificant a loss, in terms of her honour, as the loss to her life was when she killed the flea, something she has just joyfully pointed out to him:

> Just so much honor, when thou yeeld'st to mee,
> Will wast, as this flea's death tooke life from thee.
>
> (ll. 26–7)

Gender may again dictate how we respond to this conclusion but however we react, we should at the very least appreciate the poetic genius of the mind which has taken us there. And this raises an important idea in our study of the poet. Having used as his starting point a highly conventional theme, we can now see how unconventional is his treatment of it. So to what extent is this poem a love poem? If it is functioning as one, should we expect it to be seductive or persuasive? We might wish to consider whether or not Donne is perhaps more interested in the intellectual argument, the toying with ideas, than with the seduction. Adopting in our imaginations the role of the girl who is, not necessarily the object of the poem but *its recipient*, might help us decide how to answer this intriguing question. How would she have responded?

From one infamous poem we can turn now to another, and the one which employs the quintessentially metaphysical image of a compass to explore the experience of lovers parting. It is the most discussed image in the entire Donne canon and the one which so irritated Dr Johnson. *A Valediction: forbidding mourning* fits centrally into this chapter because it invites us to consider some of the most interesting questions about Donne and love poetry. Before reading it we should be aware that a valediction is a form of farewell, an address given when parting on a journey or taking leave of someone. Much has been written about the particular historical circumstances of this poem but it is far more useful at present to read the poem free from that kind of speculation. That way we can respond to it more freely and with no preconceptions. Read it carefully before continuing with the analysis here.

With the poem still fresh in our minds, we can take the opportunity to raise some fundamental questions relating to it, before making a detailed analysis. How deeply in love do the couple in the poem appear to be? Is theirs a passionate, youthful affair or a stable, well-established marriage? How important is sex in their relationship? What does the title tell us about that relationship?

We'll take the last question as our starting point because it is one that writers on Donne have neglected. 'Mourning' is a strong word. Far stronger than 'tears' or 'weeping', which might have been candidates for the situation. We mourn over death, we mourn over loss, yet this poem makes it absolutely clear through the key compass image, that this is a separation, a journey the poet is making, not a death or divorce. He is coming home again as surely and certainly as the foot of a compass will always return to its fixed partner. So from this we can safely assume that their relationship was a meaningful and serious one. Can we imagine the lover of *The Flea* or *Loves Usury* describing his partner mourning while he travelled? The poem then, deals with love of a very serious, potent kind. At this point we should refer to the critical debate which centres on whether or not the poem was written for Donne's wife, Anne, before he departed on a trip to the continent with Sir Robert Drury in 1611. The source for this idea is Izaak Walton's *Life of Dr John Donne*. It is the only poem in the entire canon which is securely dated, but Walton muddled other dates in Donne's life and only met him late in life. As so often with literature, we are left with the poem itself and should perhaps let it speak for itself.

As I have suggested, the title alone should be enough to convince us that the lovers are indeed very seriously and firmly in love with each other. A detailed analysis will confirm this. The poem opens with an analogy. The syntax of the first sentence, which straddles two verses, might be difficult to grasp at first, but if we learn from previous practice and locate the key construction which is 'As x . . . so y', it should be clear that the way virtuous men die is being compared with the way the lovers should part. How does Donne describe a virtuous man dying? That alone is interesting and should be kept in mind in later chapters when we come to study his religious poetry. Their deaths are beautifully calm, almost imperceptible. They 'whisper to their soules, to goe', and die so quietly their friends cannot even tell when they have breathed their last. Why? Because of course a good man in Donne's world knows that his reward is eternal life. We might need a little prodding to appreciate the beauty of this idea. Through his Catholic upbringing, and Calvinist conversion, Donne would have had a very intimate and purposeful relationship with death. Death in various forms pervades a great deal of his poetry, and he admits in his letters to suicidal tendencies which he had to employ the whole weight of his intellect to counter.

The same kind of beautiful, gentle, courageous parting is what he wishes for them, 'So let us melt, and make no noise'. Indeed for them to resort to 'teare-floods' or 'sigh-tempests' would be sacrilegious:

> T'were prophanation of our joyes
> To tell the layetie our love.

                                                    (ll. 7–8)

Once again we see Donne crediting his love with religious status, taking it above the comprehension of the common man, the 'layetie'.

The single-sentence third verse presents more difficulties of interpretation and it will help to isolate it before we can slot it into the poem as a whole. The first half of the sentence:

> Moving of the earth brings harms and fears;
> Men reckon what it did and meant:

                                                    (ll. 9–10)

suggests that people are troubled by the massive disruption and chaos of earthquakes, and their anxiety moves them to discover portentous meaning in such events. If we know *King Lear* we might recall Gloucester's anxious words, 'These late eclipses of the sun and moon portend no good to us.' The latter half of the sentence derives its meaning from astronomical terminology where 'trepidation' has a very specific meaning and our modern use of it is simply an obstruction. It refers to a belief in Ptolemaic astronomy that the equinoxes were affected by the vibration of the ninth or Crystalline sphere, a movement which was harmless in its ultimate effects on Earth. Having understood the sentence as it stands, it should not be so problematic now to see how it functions in the poem. Donne is still thinking of their parting and whether or not they make a grand show of it or a silent, gracious business. Donne likens their parting to the 'trepidation of the spheares': it is massive in spatial terms, 'greater farre' than even earthquakes, but is still 'innocent'. It would repay the time spent to consider for a moment the weight Donne gives that last word.

From this exalted position it is easy for him now to dismiss the 'Dull sublunary lovers love' which has mere sensuality at its core. There is something shockingly logical and impressive about Donne's point in this verse. Such lovers cannot cope with being parted, he affirms, via the near oxymoron, 'admit/ Absence' precisely *because* absence physically removes the love by removing the lovers. If we think here of the way young lovers fail so spectacularly to handle separation, of showy, clinging couples, we might begin to appreciate the essential truths underlying what Donne is writing here. To use a literary example, let Romeo and Juliet's adolescent whining about separation serve to further the point.

A lesser poet might have felt satisfied that he had made his point here through unfavourable comparison, but Donne's energy takes him on to actually attempt to describe his love. Theirs is 'so much refin'd' that they themselves can barely describe it. What they do know is that so equal and intimate is their knowledge of each other, 'Inter-assured of the mind,' that the loss of sensuality, of touch produced by parting, is less damaging to them. We should also note that 'lesse' does not dismiss the physical completely, 'Care lesse, eyes, lips, and hands to misse.'

Time spent examining the structure of this verse will enhance our growing confidence with Donne's demanding syntax. The subject of the sentence is 'we' in line 17, and although it might be straightforward to see how it links with the verbs 'refin'd' and 'know' and even 'Care' in line 20, we might have found it difficult to recognise that it also applies to 'Inter-assured of the mind'. Donne's use of ellipsis removes the 'are' we need to complete the sense before the word 'Inter-assured'.

It is here that the poem, and Donne's metaphysical mind, really takes flight. Assuring her that their love is so strong, their 'two soules . . . are one' even when he leaves, he denies that any true 'breach' will take place. Instead he finds a typically metaphysical image to impress her. Like gold leaf which has been beaten into an 'ayery thinnesse', they will experience an 'expansion' not a break. Perhaps dissatisfied with this materialistic simile after dealing with their relationship in such spiritual terms, Donne finds a far better and infamous image to finally forbid her mourning. Reread the final three verses of the poem to fix the image as a whole and find your own reponse before continuing with this analysis.

If their souls are two, they are so tightly coupled that they function like the twin legs of a 'stiff' compass. The 'stiffe' reminds us of his reluctance to leave. Remember that for Donne a compass was primarily an instrument for navigation and was symmetrical, not the pencil-bearing compasses we might be used to from childhood pencil cases. That symmetry is important because it emphasises their equality. His lover's soul becomes the fixed point of the compass, moving only to follow the other:

> Thy soule the fixt foot, makes no show
> To move, but doth, if the'other doe.

> (ll. 27–8)

Modern gender sensibilities may interfere again here, so we must appreciate that in Donne's world the wife or woman involved does not even contemplate travelling. To embark here on feminist discussions about roles is simply ludicrous and every bit as inappropriate as attempting to apply modern, non-astronomical meanings to line 11 of the poem. Donne places his woman, quite possibly his wife, at the centre here and, however far away he travels, he knows she 'leanes, and harkens after' him, wholly attached and concerned, however distant, however lengthy his absence. The last line of this verse is rich in possibilities. We know from earlier chapters that Donne is capable of obvious sexual allusion and therefore in our rereading we ought to have been aware of the punning use of 'erect' in line 32. Literally, the fixed foot of the compass straightens as the other returns, but metaphorically it grows phallically excited, anticipating the reunion. If we are following Donne's development of the image closely, something here should bring us to a halt. She is the fixed foot and there is something obviously unfitting in applying the 'erect' male pun to her. Considerable critical energy has been expended on trying to resolve not only this aspect of the image but also whether Donne is thinking of the compass drawing a circle or merely moving in a straight line back to its start.

However we choose to resolve these perceived difficulties, it is surely clear that Donne is also using 'erect' for its connotations of pride and completion and that he is differentiating in verses eight and nine about the specific movements of the compass. In verse nine he clearly wants us to think of the compass drawing a circle because he is using this image of perfection, absolute mathematical symmetry to praise his lover. If we lose sight of the truth that it is a generous and elegant love poem, we are in danger of responding to it wholly unjustly:

> Thy firmnes drawes my circle just,
> And makes me end, where I begunne.

(ll. 35–36)

The poem ends with an emphatic confirmation of fidelity and mature love. Donne will always return to her because, like the strong, central firm foot of the compass, she is his proper place, his 'home'. Perhaps now we can place more faith in Walton's statement that this poem was written for Anne More in 1611. It is quite obviously not the poem of a Romeo, or even the writer of *Elegy* XVIII. Donne has grown up.

Mature, powerful love is also the subject of *A Feaver*, the next poem to be examined here. It is reproduced completely below.

A Feaver

> Oh doe not die, for I shall hate
>   All women so, when thou art gone,
> That thee I shall not celebrate,
>   When I remember, thou wast one.
>
> But yet thou canst not die, I know,   5
>   To leave this world behinde, is death,
> But when thou from this world wilt goe,
>   The whole world vapors with thy breath.
>
> Or if, when thou, the worlds soule, goest,

It stay, tis but thy carkasse then,   10
  The fairest woman, but thy ghost,
But corrupt wormes, the worthyest men.

O wrangling schooles, that search what fire
  Shall burne this world, had none the wit
Unto this knowledge to aspire,   15
  That this her feaver might be it?

And yet she cannot wast by this,
  Nor long beare this torturing wrong,
For such corruption needfull is
  To fuell such a feaver long.   20

These burning fits but meteors bee,
  Whose matter in thee is soone spent.
Thy beauty,'and all parts, which are thee,
  Are unchangeable firmament.

Yet 'twas of my minde seising thee,   25
  Though it in thee cannot persever.
For I had rather owner bee
  Of thee one houre, than all else ever.

Of course disease, and often minor illnesses, were hurdles at which many young lives fell in early seventeenth-century London. Modern medical practice has reduced our fear of basic infections massively, so a simple fever is no longer something to be watched carefully and seen through its ferocious climax into a hopefully calm convalescence. What Donne describes in this poem is an experience which was an absolute commonplace for his contemporaries, and there are plenty of earlier poetic treatments of the idea, often in Italian, which Donne had read. Donne's originality lies in the hyperbole, the extreme exaggeration he employs to convey his feelings. We will reserve describing those feelings until later. First let us carry out the stage-by-stage analysis which is our normal practice.

The poem opens with a dramatic declaration of love and anxiety in four impressively simple words. The lady is, as can also be seen from verses four to eight, suffering the crisis of the fever, and whether she dies or survives this 'torturing wrong' is wholly uncertain. With typical overstatement, Donne turns on all womenkind in verse one. If she dies, he will have nothing but hatred for all women in future because they will remind him of her, 'When I remember, thou wast one.' We may be puzzled a little by the use of 'celebrate' in line three but he is using it in its sense of eulogising, to speak of her lovingly, after her death. Nonetheless, the entire thought is a strange one. Her death will make it impossible for him to think fondly of her, in fact it will cause him to 'hate', not a word for a religious man to use lightly. If we remind ourselves of our starting claim that the poem, like *A Valediction: forbidding mourning*, is about mature, adult love, then it makes more sense. What Donne is assuring the woman of is his fidelity. Her loss would be so devastating, there is no question of his functioning as a normal man after her death. He is writing this for his partner in life.

Faced with this crisis, he then denies the possibility of her dying at all, even though he understands death as departure from this world. He employs a favourite image, one we should be wholly familiar with by now, to make this point as powerfully as possible and in words which are beautifully apt when applied to the dramatic situation, 'The whole world vapors with thy breath.' This is a strikingly effective use of hyperbole and it leaves no room for doubt about the strength of the poet's feelings. That Donne is perfectly aware of the degree of hyperbole he is using becomes clear in the next verse, where he appears to return to reality a little to remind himself that she may very well die and he will have a whole world, full of men and women, to live in. In that case, he claims, the world she leaves behind is a mere 'carkasse', emptied of its very soul, the people on it just shadows and pitiable imitations:

> The fairest woman, but thy ghost,
>> But corrupt wormes, the worthyest men.

> (ll. 11–12)

In spite of the rhetorical form they take (this inversion of the word order is technically called a chiasmus), these are glorious compliments, and free from any hint of insincerity. But Donne has still more to give her, and turns his angry, troubled tone against the Stoic philosophers, 'wrangling schooles', who have argued about what kind of fire will consume the world. Did none of them, he asks ironically, have the intelligence to appreciate 'That this her feaver might be it?' We use the word 'wit' readily in writing about Donne and all the metaphysical poets, so it is worth appreciating here his own use of it. Clearly he locates it with intelligent thinkers and regards it as a valuable quality. It is neither trivial nor amusing.

Continuing the desperately urgent pace of the poem, Donne produces yet another magnificent compliment which a superficial reading can quite easily miss in the struggle to command the difficult syntax of verse five. He denies the evidence of his own eyes, that she is actually being wasted by this fever and enduring pain from it:

> And yet she cannot wast by this,
> Nor long beare this torturing wrong,
>
> (ll. 17–18)

because only 'corruption' could fuel such a fever. Implicit in this is the truth that she is simply beyond corruption, so how could this fever attack her? Consistently employing imagery which compares his lady with aspects of the universe, Donne dismisses the attacks of fever as 'meteors', bodies whose energy is quickly wasted. In comparison her beauty and 'all parts, which are thee', remain as firm and unalterable as the stars themselves.

The hyperbole has reached its climax, it seems, as he equates his lady with the heavens, but then Donne's agile mind adds a final brilliant stroke. Suddenly he compares himself to the fever, 'Yet 'twas of my minde, seising thee'. It thought like him when it took control of her so completely, although unlike him it will not last, 'Though it in thee cannot persever.' The simplicity and sincerity of the final lines, enhanced by the break in the rhythm after 'persever', requires little explication, and they can be allowed to speak for themselves:

> For I had rather owner bee
> Of thee one houre, than all else ever.
>
> (ll. 27–8)

Attempts to undermine the beauty of this final declaration of love by emphasising that 'seising' also has a legal sense, and 'owner' is somehow patriarchally possessive, would I think have left Donne baffled, but, more importantly, been utterly incomprehensible to the lady in question.

Now we can pick up on the question raised at the start of this analysis. How would we describe the poet's feelings here? The use of imagery is impressively coherent, the tone urgent and passionate in its bafflement and sense of imminent loss. Donne races from one idea to the next as though the crisis leaves him little time to consider, but manages nonetheless to impress on us throughout how unique and perfect his lady is. There is nothing flattering about the poem, it pours out its heart with a sincerity that rests on the brilliance of Donne's own abstract thinking to convince us. For these reasons, and in the absence of external evidence, we might sensibly wish to see something autobiographical about the poem. *A Feaver* is surely one of Donne's most eloquent love poems and is it so unreasonable to expect that it might have been written for the woman he did in fact love, his wife Anne? Perhaps a more interesting way of approaching this question is this. Would knowing for certain that it was, through historical evidence of some kind, alter our response to it? Should it? However detailed and well documented our knowledge of any writer's life and how it connects with his work, we are always left with the work itself as our own basic material. We should always work from the poem up, rather than the poet down, as it were.

The final poem we shall examine under 'The Intensity of Love' heading is *The Extasie*. appropriately one of his most demanding and controversial poems. Before reading it we need to make yet another lexical realignment. For a modern student 'ecstasy' is a word loaded with unwanted baggage. We need to dump all of that and use it in the mystical sense Donne's readers would have done. It is a state of rapture or heightened sensitivity which has a religious content to it. The soul leaves the body and is free to contemplate the divine. Now read the poem carefully. If in the edition of Donne's poetry you are using it is printed as one verse, try reading it as though it were in quatrains, like *A Valediction: forbidding mourning*, which is how some editors have chosen to print it.

Before addressing some of the controversy surrounding the poem, we need to have a clear appreciation of the dramatic situation and how it progresses. Even that is difficult in this uncompromisingly abstract poem. We begin with two lovers sitting on a grassy bank. Words like 'bed, 'Pregnant', 'pillow' and 'swel'ed' combine to create a mood of sexual expectation. Violets are also flowers with strong associations of fidelity in love, and in some sources are closely connected to the goddess of love, Venus. We might also profit from deciding what we think the initial description of the lovers as 'one anothers best' suggests about their relationship up to this point. They hold hands 'firmely' and whatever is happening between them causes 'a fast balme' to 'spring' from their hands and bind them even closer. A 'balme' would most commonly be taken to describe some kind of natural, soothing ointment, frequently with a fragrance. The imagery then takes a typically metaphysical turn as Donne conceives their mutually engaged looks twisted together on some imaginary line or 'string'. Considerable critical energy has again been exercised here but, instead of summarising the various ingenious positions, I would prefer you to make your own mind up about how this conceit strikes you. Its vocabulary does not require any extraneous knowledge or reading and its originality almost demands we treat it with respect. However we might respond, we should conclude somewhere that Donne is certainly intent on stressing how rapt the lovers are.

The confusion over the next quatrain 'So to'entergraft . . . . . . propagation' (ll. 9–10) may be lessened if instead of fixing on a meaning for 'to'entergraft', we simply appreciate that both 'to'entergraft' and 'propogation' are, in reproductive terms, entirely consistent with the opening words we decided were full of sexual potential. As yet, Donne is saying, what is happening between them is not sexual. Need we really look elsewhere for the meaning of 'Was all the means to make us one'? There has been no mention at all yet of the unification of their *souls*. It is only after a first reading that this becomes a hindrance. The dramatic situation is what we should focus on, and Donne presents us with two lovers, out of doors, in a private and romantic setting. It is also useful to compare it with the same situation in *The Flea*. What is different here is what most assists our understanding. This girl is not the least bit reluctant. In fact she is as equally excited and involved as the poet. To deny that sexual intercourse is on his mind here has to be one of the most naive readings of love poetry imaginable. It is also worth noting the similarity with *The Good-Morrow* where 'My face in thine eye, thine in mine appeares' (l. 15). And in the next quatrain we have further confirmation that this experience is not a sexual one, or at least not yet.

As equally balanced armies endure a time of uncertain victory, so the lovers' souls endure a period of balanced uncertainty. The use of battle as a metaphor for love-making is entirely conventional, but Donne is more concerned here with the balance than with the struggle. It is here that the uniqueness of this whole event, this ecstasy, is asserted by Donne most strikingly. As their two souls 'negotiate there', they lie as still and as silent as stone statues on tombs, 'All day'. (As fine an example of hyperbole in Donne as one could wish to find.) What we should again draw from this is the stress Donne places on their lack of physical involvement. They are both still and silent. It is their souls that speak.

A third party now hypothetically enters the scene. The essential aspect of this third party that we must grasp, whatever we might feel about his being a Platonic lover or not, is that he understands their 'soules language'. There is also a consistency in the imagery here drawn from metallurgy. This third party is 'refin'd' by love, and by lines 27–8 he has been so much refined that he leaves 'farre purer than he came.' The term 'concoction' in line 27 has a specific chemical meaning and describes the purifying of substances by heat. Gold was believed to be concocted by the the sun underground. What Donne really wants us to believe is that this listener to their souls learns something astoundingly precious from them. He also makes sure we have understood the souls are so completely in communion, that they speak with one voice. That voice is what we are then privileged to hear for ourselves:

This Extasie doth unperplex
(We said) and tell us what we love,
We see by this, it was not sexe,

(ll. 29–31)

It makes absolute sense, as some editors do by adding speech marks, to then treat all which follows to the end of the poem as the single voice of their combined souls in ecstasy.

The first thing their souls notice is that the ecstatic experience is a demystifying one. It allows them to see that it was not sex which brought them together but something far greater. The difficult line 32 is another example of simple ellipsis, and placing 'that' after 'see' should resolve any confusion. They now know that before this they had no idea what had moved them to love. A glance at verse five of *A Valediction: forbidding mourning* shows us a closely allied thought. Secondly, they understand that just as every soul is a mixture of things unknown to it, so love mixes these mixtures of souls again until both become one, 'each this and that'. This latter phrase is unusually vague, but appears to confirm that their two souls become one so completely that they are indistinguishable.

Returning to the violet as an appropriate emblem, Donne now produces a notoriously obscure passage. The most practical way to approach it is to separate the following eight lines into two quatrains linked by analogy:

> A single violet transplant,
>   The strength, the colour, and the size,
> (All which before was poore, and scant,)
>   Redoubles still and multiplies.

(ll. 37–40)

What he appears to want us to believe is that the moving of a violet from one place to another does not weaken or undo it in any way. What does happen is that naturally it improves its colour, vigour and size. It may help to separate the 'single violet' from the verb 'redoubles' which applies only to 'strength,' 'colour' and 'size'. Any gardener will know that violets are free-spreading and will propagate themselves freely, especially in a new site, and this may reduce the urge to torture this obscure passage any further. We can then examine the next quatrain as an analogy:

> When love, with one another so
> Interanimates two soules,

That abler soule, which thence doth flow,
Defects of lonelinesse controules.

(ll. 41–4)

Concentrating on the enjambement (the fluency) between lines 41 and 42 can help us to a clearer reading in which the 'abler soule' becomes like the transplanted violet, stronger, richer, healthier and more beautiful. More time debating these confusing lines is best kept for the seminar or classroom.

The poem then confirms the existence of the new soul which, once fully aware of its own composition, asserts its invulnerability in line 48, 'whom no change can invade'. The exclamatory 'But O alas', which begins the next line, is good reason for us to summarise the dramatic position so far, before the new influx of ideas begins. Drawn together by their love, the lovers find themselves alone and in silent communication quite new to them both. So rapt are they, their souls leave their bodies and communicate so intimately, ecstatically, that they become one new soul which brings them both to a richer, clearer understanding of their love and how superior it is to the ordinary experience of love. This soul speaks to them both in one, heightened voice.

Resist the temptation to echo his 'But O alas', if from this incredible height of spiritual abstraction you suspect the poem is taking a well-known and predictable route. How do we respond now to the question which follows?

But O alas, so long, so farre
Our bodies why doe wee forbeare?

(ll. 49–50)

To what extent do we sense anticlimax? And if we do start to think we know what is about to come, why do we think that way? Are we so obviously once again waist-deep in a poem of seduction? Has all this almost outrageously abstract debate been just another a ploy to bed another girl, this time on flowers? We must reserve judgement and continue the analysis.

He begins the new line of thinking by distinguishing between their bodies and themselves. 'They are ours, though they are not wee.' For Donne the existence of the soul is without question. What he does question is its nature and how we can find ways to discuss and describe it. We might be ardent Darwinians, but that does not affect Donne's debate in the slightest and we have to respect the intellectual and scientific environment in which it takes place. In fact without some knowledge of it we cannot truly understand key passages like the one which follows. It was believed that angels controlled the spheres, and Donne compares the relation of the lovers to their bodies, to angels and their spheres. The point of the comparison is clear. The body is the active, physical form the individual takes, while the soul guides it like the controlling angel guides the sphere. For this reason, he then argues, the lovers must thank their bodies because without them they would never have met. It was through their physical being that they first came to know each other and love each other in this ecstatic manner. The logic here is indisputable (as so often when Donne seems intent on seduction).

The insistence in the tone is heightened by repetition in lines 54–6, as he concludes this section of his debate by picking up on the metallurgical imagery to insist their bodies are like 'allay' not 'drosse'. The former (alloy) is an addition to a metal which usually strengthens it or increases its value, the latter is the waste product from any metal-refining process. It is a subtle refinement to the argument begun at line 51. Cosmological scholarship again comes into play as Donne uses the way in which celestial bodies influence man only by moving the air first, as his image for the way one soul may influence another, only via the body first:

> Soe soule into the soule may flow,
>   Though it to body first repaire.

(ll. 59–60)

We have learned from longer poems how to analyse difficult sentences as single units, and the next sentence is a complex one, but our earlier hint to read the poem in quatrains is equally helpful here. The structure of this passage then becomes much more obvious as shown now:

As our blood labours to beget
  Spirits, as like soules as it can,
Because such fingers need to knit
  The subtile knot, which makes us man;

So must pure lovers soules descend
  T'affections, and to faculties,
Which sense may reach and apprehend,
  Else a great Prince in prison lies.

                                        (ll. 61–8)

The bold words signal the structure and allow us to deal with each
verse separately and then to link them as they should be linked,
analogously. The first verse here relies on contemporary medical
science which variously held that 'Spirits' were an immensely rarified
liquid or vapour in the blood which enabled the soul to make the
body act, and conveyed sensation from the body to the soul. The
second applies this principle to the lovers and their need to revert to
their bodies ultimately to feel emotion and to act on that emotion.

   This is in one sense the climax of the poem, and a phrase which
has understandably intrigued critics on Donne. Is the 'great Prince'
Love, or is it the soul? Does Donne's ecstatic soul, which we must
remember is speaking, claim that they must return now to their
single bodies and souls to make love, or else they are abusing some-
thing magnificent and central to the state of happiness? Or does it
merely remind itself that they cannot function properly as human
beings, with individual souls, unless they return to them singly, this
day of ecstasy having been just one mystical stage in their deepening
love?

   The abstract and even abstruse arguments may well have dis-
tanced us from the poem by now so we should take stock and reflect
on what Donne may have achieved. Rereading the poem to line 68
can help us.

   The end-stopped line 68 is obviously emphatic and undoubtedly
Donne is eager to drive this point home. A glance back at what
immediately precedes it helps. He chooses the word 'descend' to
mark the way their souls return to their bodies, clearly because he
views the shift from this ecstasy as a step down. But it is an unavoid-

able step if life is to continue in any meaningful fashion. One aid to our understanding is to appreciate that Donne uses 'sense' in line 67, not 'mind' or 'heart' or anything similarly vague. He means it. Without our bodies we cannot live, never mind love:

> To'our bodies turne wee then, that so
> Weake men on love reveal'd may looke;
> Love's mysteries in soules doe grow,
> But yet the body is his booke.

(ll. 69–72)

Can we really still deny now that the poem contains a plea for sexual union? Donne might well have felt so confident and close to his lover that he could imagine their soul's voice becoming one, but how much more persuasive is it to actually assume that, and place his own words on her tempted lips. When they do as he suggests and return to their bodies, they are almost semi-divine. It is for 'Weake men' to admire them, and although the spiritual aspects of love do rest in souls, you cannot read them, indeed know anything of them at all, unless you use the body as a book. And I'm sure in Donne's imagination it is a fascinating and vast tome.

Returning finally to the idea of the third party witnessing all this, Donne concludes the poem by reassuring the girl, though with none of the brilliance of *The Flea* or *A Feaver*. The observer, having heard their united soul in 'dialogue of one' (itself a deft paradox), will not be able to see any change in them once they have 'to bodies gone'. He assumes, not surprisingly since the debate has never been a true dialogue, that she will be eager to start her reading and they will sleep together.

This concludes our detailed analysis, but is really only the starting point for serious critical discussion. Ezra Pound called the poem 'Platonism believed', a far cry from my analysis here. Is *The Extasie* a frivolous, elaborate, ingenious attempt at seduction, or is it a sincere and brilliantly incisive attempt to describe one experience of love in metaphysical terms?

We can return now to the questions we set ourselves at the start of this chapter and draw some conclusions. As the discoveries we are now making are more complex, those conclusions cannot really take the segregated form they did in the first two chapters.

How far does Donne detail the experience of love or just reflect on it? If he does detail it at all it is from an unapologetically selfish viewpoint. The closest he comes to placing himself in his lover's shoes is to allow the girl of *The Flea* some voice of her own. Even *A Feaver* comes from, is driven by, his fears and his responses to her illness. Nonetheless, the ferocity and potency of the urge itself, the desire for love and the pleasures of love, pervade great swathes of his verse in spite of his efforts to intellectualise the experience.

How far and for what reasons does he employ eulogy? Once again we end up reading love poems, apparently to individual women, with little or no sense at all of what they are like. Yet the extent of his praise is often devastating and in some poems like *A Valediction: forbidding mourning*, and *A Feaver*, there seems ample evidence for us to think the poems were written for his wife, which goes some way to answering our question about how autobiographical his work is. Certainly Donne never actively strains to associate himself with the poetry, not at all surprising when we recall he regarded writing poetry as something like an embarrassing habit he could not quite shake off. In his letters he is always dismissive when complimented, and, however defensive this may have been, in comparison to many modern writers, he is laconic indeed on the subject of his own poetry.

Finally, can his meditations on love communicate effectively with readers today? Donne is a difficult poet and difficulty is not in vogue. In a culture where visual imagery supercedes every other kind, writing as intense as Donne's is virtually anathema to the majority. Yet to the student of literature he remains one of the most stimulating, original exponents of English poetry they are ever likely to encounter. Love fascinated him and fired his poetic imagination. If we can surmount the few scientific and cosmological allusions which pepper the *Songs and Sonnets*, we should find ourselves in communication with one of the most abrasive, persistent minds ever to have attempted to understand this most baffling of human experiences.

Suggested Work

- Read *Loves Growth*, putting it to the same close scrutiny to decide how it works as a love poem. Does it add to our understanding of the nature of love? Are there ideas in it which we have already encountered in this chapter?

- Put *The Dreame* to precisely the same examination and then compare it with *Love's Growth* from the point of view of the recipient.

4

Confusion and Doubt

Some writers on Donne have made much of the unstable and shifting nature of his verse. John Carey describes him as 'fiercely schizoid'[1] and any analysis of his work which did not take into account those poems which overtly exhibit this tendency would be failing its readers. In this chapter we will be analysing some of those poems and trying to cope with their unsettling effects. In many of them what we find is Donne openly grappling with the ideas himself. Perhaps one of his strongest and most hotly disputed qualities is this readiness to admit his own confusion, and to include it in his verse. It is, after all, far easier to walk away from confusion than confront it with hard thinking. Donne not only acknowledges difficult thought, he articulates it. *The Prohibition* is a valuable place to start this chapter because it is so self-consciously puzzling and confusing. Even the wording and structural use of repetition challenges the reader to keep up. It is reproduced below.

The Prohibition

Take heed of loving mee
At least remember, I forbade it thee;
Not that I shall repaire my'unthrifty wast
Of Breath and Blood, upon thy sighes, and teares,
By being to thee then what to mee thou wast;   5
But, so great Joy, our life at once outweares,
Then, lest thy love, by my death, frustrate bee,
If thou love mee, take heed of loving mee.

Take heed of hating mee,   10
Or too much triumph in the Victorie.
Not that I shall be mine owne officer,
And hate with hate again retaliate;
But thou wilt lose the stile of conquerour,
If I, thy conquest, perish by thy hate.   15
Then, lest my being nothing lessen thee,
If thou hate mee, take heed of hating mee.

Yet, love and hate mee too,
So, these extreames shall neithers office doe;
Love mee, that I may die the gentler way;   20
Hate mee, because thy love is too great for mee;
Or let these two, themselves, not me decay;
So shall I, live, thy Stage, not triumph bee;
Lest thou thy love and hate and mee undoe,
To let mee live, O love and hate mee too.   25

'Take heed' is an outdated warning meaning something like beware. The title itself is forceful and the imperative used in the opening phrase establishes an angry, accusatory tone from the start. Donne is evidently upset by his lover's coldness, as is confirmed in lines 3 and 4, where he speaks of his having wasted both 'Breath and Blood, upon thy sighes, and teares'. Clearly she is not returning his affections. He reminds her that he warned her not to love him, but is aware that should she love him now, it would not make up for that waste. The sense of 'repaire' in line 3 is closer to the modern 'compensate for', or 'recover', and his use of 'unthrifty' implies self-criticism and resentment. If line 5 proves resistant, we can clarify things by the simple formula 'Not that I shall repaire' . . . x with 'By being' . . . y in line 5, a method we used in Chapter 2. (But note there is no corresponding 'by' to go with the 'but' of line six.) The meaning ought then to be much easier to follow. Whatever his feelings for her now, he assures her his love for her is over by using the past tense and an emphatic pause to end line 5.

The riddling nature of the poem becomes overtly clear in the last three lines of the verse. If we take line 6 to simply highlight that shared love, 'great Joy', exhausts them, we can separate the final couplet off. In case her love for him is frustrated by his premature death, Donne repeats his opening warning with the infuriating addition, 'If thou love mee'. It is infuriating because we know it is not simply repetition and requires some thought. The extra baggage it carries shifts the meaning very subtly. If we try to read it literally we end up with a pointless qualification. If you love me, then beware of . . . loving me! What Donne is doing by this overt use of repetition is deliberately challenging his reader to think more deeply. What are the possible ways he might be using the qualifying phrase? One is suggested here. There is a sense in which 'If thou love mee', has a very conventional ironic meaning, as a hopeful appeal to the other's sense of duty or responsibility, and not really their love. The sense is something more akin to 'If you have any respect for me at all', because the speaker *knows* love is not being given. Donne has told us this in extremely forceful terms already, and this ironic sense may well be the most effective.

The riddling tone is reinforced at the start of the second verse by the antithesis of line 1, 'Take heed of hating mee.' A very natural response to this use of opposites is to ask, well what on earth does he want her to do? Donne's tone stimulates us to question. He warns her not to relish her 'Victorie' over him too much, not because he will respond to her hatred with hatred of his own, line 12, but because if she destroys him by her neglect then she has lost the claim to be his 'conquerour,' and the satisfaction which goes with it. Donne's use of 'officer' in line 11 is problematic, but if we think of an officer as acting for someone, on their behalf, in a legal or even military sense, we should have a clearer understanding.

The step he takes to end the second verse is logical but entirely specious. He advises her against hating him once more, since, if his death is the result, a dramatic claim by anyone's standards, her standing will suffer as a result. The verse ends, again very logically, with a precise antithesis of line 8 but the riddling is far from over as the final verse turns everything he has previously requested around. 'Yet, love and hate mee too', he pleads. Once more we are encouraged to question why, and he quickly answers that this will neutralise these 'extreames'. Sensing he has her full attention now, having virtually baffled her into it, Donne now addresses the girl with what he wants her to believe is an honest heart, the simplicity and directness of 'Love mee' and 'Hate mee' in lines 19 and 20 claim that response.

He asks to be loved so that he 'may die the gentler way', which implies through the joy of being loved by her or simply generates a sexual pun on 'die', to experience an orgasm. His request for her hate should cause us to stop and think a little more. On one level he uses these two demands to reject the deaths imagined in verse one and verse two respectively. But the claim in line 20 that 'thy love is too great for mee', comes as something of a surprise after so much apparent bitterness and anger. It is a compliment, and one so placed as to have the most effect. Let both love and hate 'themselves' die rather than destroy me, he asks next, as this will bring its reward.

Line 22 is editorially one of the most contentious, and different editors attempt to resolve the difficulty in various ingenious ways. Our version is one of the simplest. In this way, he states, he remains alive to be a constant proof of her worth and value; her 'Stage' rather than her one-off 'triumph'. What else we might wish to make of his use of 'Stage' to describe his role in their future relationship is again worth consideration in the seminar or classroom. But the warning tone of the poem has not been abandoned and he resumes it in the penultimate line, placing the onus firmly on her. It is her behaviour that threatens to destroy her, her love, her hate and himself, 'Lest thou thy love and hate and mee undoe.' The line is as compact and condensed as any in the *Songs and Sonnets* , and cleverly brings the riddling to a climax as Donne ends with one more tantalising invitation to the reader (and of course the girl) to work out what he wants.

'To let mee live, O love and hate mee too.'

Trying to force a single meaning onto a line which is so obviously designed to provoke is simply an inappropriate response, as it is to the poem as a whole. Part of Donne's technique here is to use density, ambiguity and wit, to stimulate his reader. We should appreciate that and enjoy being teased. It would be an antiseptic mind indeed, that failed to see this is an entirely appropriate way for a love poem to work, and a love poet to behave.

From a deliberately puzzling poem to one which, on first reading, might not strike us as especially doubtful or confused: *Womans Constancy* is a single verse which uses a number of rhetorical questions to provoke its imaginary recipient and the reader into a response.

Womans Constancy

Now thou hast lov'd me one whole day,
To morrow when thou leav'st, what wilt thou say?
Wilt thou then Antedate some new made vow?
    Or say that now
We are not just those persons, which we were?   5
Or, that oathes made in reverentiall feare
Of Love, and his wrath, any may forsweare?
Or, as true deaths, true maryages untie,
So lovers contracts, images of those,
Binde but till sleep, deaths image, them unloose?   10
    Or, your owne end to Justifie,
For having purpos'd change, and falsehood; you
Can have no way but falsehood to be true?
Vaine lunatique, against these scapes I could
    Dispute, and conquer, if I would,   15
    Which I abstaine to doe,
For by to morrow, I may thinke so too.

Our usual method is to carry out a detailed analysis before considering the poem's overall effect or possible responses to it. This poem raises an intriguing question which prevents us from doing that as freely as before. We will address that question first and then proceed with the analysis hand in hand with other issues which arise from it. The poem is titled *Womans Constancy* but details a woman's betrayal of a man. If the poet's voice is male, he is complaining about a woman's *inconstancy*. The key question concerns the gender of the poetic voice. Our assumption that it is male comes solely from our knowing the poet is Donne. Read the poem with a woman's voice or a man's, and it makes perfect sense in either case. Indeed, read as the former, the title makes far more sense. If this is a woman speaking, the poem becomes a eulogy to women and their fidelity. If a man, it becomes a misogynistic diatribe – quite different things in the world of literary criticism. There is, of course, a third possibility which our analysis of *The Prohibition* might have already triggered.

That the lovers are not married is evident from line 8 but that they have been deeply involved, possibly even sexually, is equally evident from lines 6 and 7. The poem begins with a reference to time which at first appears a little unhelpful, 'one whole day' seems merely a means of underlining the fickleness of the departing lover. If the speaker is female, this makes more sense because we are far more used conventionally to the faithless male, especially if the opening line implies that their love has just involved sex for the first time. In view of our awareness of Donne's fondness for poems of seduction, we can readily imagine here the sense of imminent abandonment a girl who has finally acceded to sex after a lengthy and insistent courtship might feel. In either case, the lover sensing the danger of abandonment, wonders rhetorically what the faithless one will say and then produces five separate answers, all but the first commencing with 'Or', which we can examine in turn.

Firstly, will they lie and say their newly made vow was made at an earlier date? Secondly, will they pretend they are, purely due to the passage of time, different people from the ones who swore love to each other? The third answer imagines the faithless lover denying the sincerity of the vows they made, if not under God's eyes, as a marriage, under Love's. The fourth builds on the reference to marriage and suggests they will say that just as real death undoes real marriage, so lovers' vows, which are images of true marriages, are binding only till the next night when sleep, like death, undoes them. It is a typically witty use of analogy and is expressed with deft elegance. The fifth and final deceitful reply captures something far more telling and eschews analogy to do it. Trying to justify their action in pursuing their selfish ends, ironically change and falsehood become the only true means they have to act. The paradoxical 'Can have no way but falsehood to be true?' brings the list of imagined responses to an end, but whatever the gender of the speaker, these are wonderfully incisive observations of human behaviour. Men and women can be inventively adept at justifying the most outrageous or blatant betrayals.

A powerful caesura in line 14 marks the shift in tone which the poem now employs to conclude its poignant complaint. 'Vaine lunatique,' he or she sighs (and vanity is not an exclusively female weakness). Against such vacuous excuses ('scapes') they could easily argue, and win if they chose to, but they do not. Donne reserves the most potent thought till last. For by the next day, they too might have fallen out of love.

However we choose to read the poem, from a male or female perspective, it is a beautifully touching and melancholy capturing of that moment when one lover recognises that they are now unloved and the immediate future is sickeningly bleak. In its conclusion it is a pragmatic and poignantly human acceptance of the sad truth that love can end, and sadder still, even the unsullied, courageous constancy of the spurned can be undone by time. If we now look at the 'one whole day' of line 1 and the 'to morrow' of line 17 as representative rather than specific, we should be able to see the beautifully rounded design Donne gives the whole.

Our third possibility is that it is quite possible that the uncertain gender of the poetic voice is deliberate. It would of course have been a simple matter to make it clear but the poem doesn't. Throughout, the terms remain interchangeable, and why that doubt was retained by Donne is once more something which may well be valuable fuel for discussion outside the pages of this study.

The dramatic situation of the next poem in this chapter is, like *The Flea*, not original to Donne. *The Apparition* describes how a rejected lover will return to haunt his mistress, and many earlier poets had also imagined the satisfaction to be gained in such an impossible situation. It is reproduced below.

The Apparition

When, by thy scorne, O murdresse, I am dead,
And that thou thinkst thee free
From all solicitation from mee,
Then shall my ghost come to thy bed,

And thee, fain'd vestall, in worse armes shall see;   5
Then thy sick taper will begin to winke,
And he, whose thou art then, being tyr'd before,
Will, if thou stirre, or pinch to wake him, thinke
    Thou call'st for more,
And in false sleepe will from thee shrinke,   10
And then poore Aspen wretch, neglected thou
Bath'd in a cold quicksilver sweat wilt lye
    A veryer ghost than I;
What I will say, I will not tell thee now,
Lest that preserve thee'; and since my love is spent,   15
I'had rather thou shouldst painfully repent,
Than by my threatnings rest still innocent.

A first reading should be sufficient for us to appreciate the overall tone and key thoughts in the poet's mind. But the poem repays deeper analysis and prompts some intriguing doubts and uncertainties. We begin with the poet imagining it is the girl's 'scorn' which has killed him – not at all unusual for Donne to think, and something we have recently observed in *The Prohibition*. The French have a saying which goes something like 'To die for love is overdoing the thing.' Donne is one of the most hyperbolic poets in the English language and is frequently driven to extremes in an effort to make himself understood. Hardly surprising then that he finds the idea of dying from love not in the least strained. *The Apparition* opens unequivocally with this claim, as though it is a certainty, not an inflated piece of poetic rhetoric. 'When, by thy scorn, O murdresse, I am dead' allows us now room for manoeuvre. His death will happen, and her disdain for him will be the cause. If we remind ourselves of the tactic we have used before of imagining ourselves the recipient of the poem, this claim is hardly something we could ignore. If it doesn't appeal to our sense of realism, it is likely to appeal to our vanity.

Donne then capitalises quickly on this shock tactic in the next two lines. By acknowledging her confident belief that she is now safe from his attentions, 'all solicitation from mee,' he is subtly showing her that he knows her mind and how she thinks, which is another ingenious encouragement to hold the girl's attention. That is the point at which he will visit her as a ghost, and Donne takes some delight in timing this visit to suit her own delightful activities. Arriving at her bedside he discovers her in a new, obviously inferior, lover's arms. The phrase 'fain'd vestall' may require some explanation because both words are not in common usage today. Vestal virgins attended at the temple of Vesta in ancient Rome and 'fain', as an adjective, means eager or willing, although a modern reader is quite likely to hear the homonym, 'feigned'. Of course Donne is punning too, and satirically hinting that not only is the girl an eager participant in bed, but she is skilful enough to fake virginity for the benefit of this new lover. It is an important detail to appreciate because it so strongly affects the tone of the poem. Again Donne's intimate knowledge of the girl is stressed.

The satire continues as he pictures the thin candle she has as a night light in her room, a 'taper', guttering and failing as his ghost disturbs the atmosphere. Still absolutely confident of her reactions and response, he then imagines her trying to wake her lover who has fallen asleep before her after their love-making. However, with a rare touch of uncomplicated humour, he describes the new lover faking sleep because he thinks her pinches and attempts to wake him are clarion calls to further sexual gymnastics, and the work-out she has already given him has left him exhausted:

> And he, whose thou art then, being tyr'd before,
> Will, if thou stirre, or pinch to wake him, thinke
>   Thou call'st for more,
> And in false sleepe will from thee shrinke,
>
> (ll. 7–10)

The climactic satisfaction Donne's ghost feels is obvious as it now observes its former lover shaking and trembling with fear, bathed in a cold sweat, more ghost than Donne himself. There are two words which might hinder an easy reading of these few lines. 'Aspen' refers to a type of tree which has especially tremulous leaves. The analogy is a highly conventional one in literature and not at all original to Donne. The second word is 'quicksilver' which is another term for mercury, the bizarrely fluid metal which Donne uses here to describe the beads of cold sweat which gather on the girl's face or body.

Having reduced her to a shivering wreck in his imagination, Donne shows a little mercy by stopping short of telling her now what he will say then as a ghost. But being merciful is not his intention. His reluctance to speak now is in fact ingeniously designed to keep her in fear of his visitation, 'lest that preserve thee', where 'that' refers to his choice speech. If he were to speak now, she could 'rest still innocent' because she would know what he will say, but by holding his tongue he hopes to make her 'painfully repent'. Has he maintained the bitter tone to the end? Initially we might answer with a confident 'yes', but is it so straightforward? If we ask ourselves what he hoped to achieve by the poem we may find a different answer, one which is dependent on the intimacy he has assumed throughout. The poem takes as undeniable their former intimacy. It adopts a hurt, cruel and almost gloating tone which ends by openly acknowledging its own posturing, 'threatenings'. Yet the humour of the central dramatic moment, the exhausted new lover pretending to be asleep because he cannot cope with her sexual appetite, may also be seen as an intimate, generous compliment. Donne can only say all this from experience of her.

If that is the case, there is scope to view the poem very comfortably within the *Songs and Sonnets* as a whole as a love poem. What Donne wants is not to punish her or insult all women via her: he just wants her back.

As an antidote to *The Prohibition* and *The Apparition*, read *Lovers Infinitenesse*. After reading it, you may well see immediately that it is a strikingly different poem and demonstrates the kind of shocking shift of sensibility which gives writers on Donne attacks of the vapours. Are they really from the same pen, or more acutely, mind? They are, and understanding this is the chief aim of this chapter. *Lovers Infinitenesse* contains a wealth of material for the serious student of Donne and, in spite of the few serious textual difficulties, it rises way above them to become extremely accessible. It is equally stimulating if juxtaposed with other poems, which is why we have placed it here in this chapter and subjected it to the usual detailed analysis.

Before embarking on the analysis it is worth pointing out that some editions have the poem written as three single sentences corresponding to the three verses, others place additional full stops at lines 6 and 19. In either case, the way in which the complicated syntax becomes almost unnoticeable, gently smothered by some of Donne's most fluent verse, is a remarkable achievement. There is a clever combination in the poem of simple, near colloquial diction, with extremely skilful versification. If we were to compare it with Wordsworth's *Lyrical Ballads*, recalling his ideal to use 'the language of ordinary men', the comparison might be very telling.

The open, intensely personal tone is established immediately through the simple diction and direct second-person address:

> If yet I have not all thy love
> Deare, I shall never have it all,

(ll. 1–2)

Yet it leaves us wondering because of the doubt expressed about her capacity to love. Donne explains in the next four lines that his own efforts to gain her love have been exhausted. All the formal weapons of the conventional suitor, 'Sighes, teares and oathes, and letters' have failed to elicit from her all her love. Donne is spent – not such an inappropriate term as we might think, as Donne implies it himself by using 'treasure' and 'purchase' in line 5. In this first section of the poem, which in our edition is a single sentence, we should recognise a familiar figure. But this unhappy lover sounds neither bitter nor angry. The endearment in line 2 and the gentle fluency of the verse which places a heavy cadence on 'fall' in line 4, convince us of this. A similar effect comes from the lengthy, drawn out, melancholy sound of 'Sighs, teares, and oathes, and letters I have spent.' If we read these opening lines aloud, and at least one of Donne's famous editors has complained of the absence of skill amongst his students in this respect, we ought to be able to hear most effectively that intensely personal, melancholy tone.

Continuing the argument, Donne then reminds himself that this expectation is itself wholly unrealistic because whatever 'bargaine' they struck between them, initially, set the parameters of their love. How then could he expect more? Pursuing the thought ingeniously, he assumes for the argument's sake that her original 'gift of love' was incomplete, that she had always imagined sharing her love. If so, he reflects, sadly, but with impeccable logic, he will never have all of her love. The use of 'Deare' once more stresses that he is neither angry nor bitter.

The movement his thought takes in verse two is entirely typical because of its restless insistence. It is as though Donne simply cannot resist thinking, per se. The urge to understand drives him forwards, forcing him to examine every imaginable angle and twist to the debate. So he now adopts the opposite position, imagining the consequences if she has given him all her love already. With some deftness he raises his hopes by asserting that 'all' is subject to time, and 'all' then does not prevent the capacity for growth at all. She may well have a greater capacity for love now than at their original 'bargaine'.

It is a short step from this increasingly negative perspective to imagine that not only will she be able to make new men love her, but they may well be able to inspire love in her, their armouries being largely intact and more effective than his. Donne consistently employs the language of commerce to describe this process, bringing an element of harsh realism into the debate:

> But if in thy heart, since, there be or shall,
> New love created bee, by other men,
> Which have their stocks intire, and can in teares,
> In sighs, in oathes, and letters outbid mee,
>
> (ll. 14–17)

He acknowledges that this situation would increase his anxiety and then, building on his use of 'beget' in line 18, his thoughts leap rapidly to challenge the idea that this new love was never 'vowed', and presumably therefore has less validity than theirs. 'And yet it was,' he counters, because if her gift of love was not specific to him but 'generall,' none the less her heart remains his and like earth he has tilled himself, whatever grows there should by rights be his. The shifting, uncertain volatility of the thinking is baffling to a reader lulled by the gentle tone and rhythm. By the end of the second verse, Donne has moved from a starting point where he accepts the impossibility of having all her love, to one where he insists all her love is his by right.

If there were no third verse, our habitual susceptibility to completion might well allow us to be entirely satisfied with the poem at line 22. There would be a rounded neatness about it which would make sense. But Donne, of course, does not stop there. The slippery little word 'Yet' engages us once more and introduces a startlingly new note of uncertainty. Donne abruptly denies wanting all of her love, 'Yet I would not have all yet.' The intellectual control he has over his verse is sometimes very visible in his ingenious use of structure on any scale, and here we can see this single, apparently simple line is actually shaped by the same monosyllabic word, 'yet', although he is changing its meaning. A leap of razor-edged wit explains his new position. If he has all of her love already, he can logically have no more, and as his own love for her is growing daily, she should expect greater 'rewards' from him. With similar crystalline logic he adds that it is an impossibility for her to give him her heart each day, since if she still has it to give, she must never have parted with it.

The subsequent lines about 'Loves riddles' are far from clear and have a number of possible interpretations. The use of 'riddles' alone alerts us to this, and undoubtedly Donne is provoking his reader. To be left puzzled and searching for meaning here is, then, a wholly appropriate sensation, and we should resist critics or teachers who insist on forcing a single, sensible version onto us. Logically, and logic has figured highly in the poem so far, there ought to be two riddles separated by the 'and' of line 30. The first requires us to explain how she can keep and lose her heart simultaneously: the second how she can save her heart by losing it. Possibly the most valuable way to reach some conclusions, however tentative, is to raise these issues in a classroom or seminar where several minds can contribute. Whatever we conclude, both riddles reassure the girl, and imply a deepening of their love will strengthen it. The resigned, sad tone of the earlier verses has been inched out to be replaced by something markedly more optimistic.

'But wee will have a way more liberall,' is completely assured and determined in tone. There is no longer a question about this, they 'will' find a more 'liberall' or generous way, a way of loving far superior to the one threatened by 'other men', in verse two. But the provocative, uncertain tone of the poem is not entirely extinguished. Does 'changing' in line 32 suggest alteration, novelty or reassessment? Or is it merely an abbreviated version of exchanging? Is the ambiguity deliberate? Whatever we decide, we can not ignore the ringing confidence and faith of these final lines, or the simple beauty of his desire:

> . . . so we shall
> Be one, and one anothers All.

(ll. 32–3)

Having analysed *Lovers Infinitenesse* and discovered a ruthlessly logical sequence of steps in an argument, clothed in the language of immensely tender, personal address, we can place it alongside the other poems in this chapter and appreciate why Donne infuriated some of his critics. If we discover how alert his intellect is, we are likely to be frustrated to find him changing his mind or contradicting himself in different poems. And yet, as I hope we have been gradually appreciating in this chapter, the foundation of the *Songs and Sonnets*, even in poems which may superficially seem misogynistic or bitter, is as love poetry. Fundamentally Donne is writing to seduce, or praise, or express his love as potently as possible. *Lovers Infinitenesse* is a superb example of this. We might even see Donne scaling new heights in a poem like this because it so skilfully unites sincerity with intellect, form with feeling. We may recall observations we made about his earlier work in Chapters 1 and 2, which highlighted his tendency virtually to ignore the loved one as he became bound up in his own thoughts. If we nurture this idea too closely, we will find it difficult to explain poems like *Lovers Infinitenesse* or the next poem under scrutiny, *The Anniversarie*. Maturity is an obvious explanation, and perhaps fidelity might play a part. What scraps of information we have about his courtship and marriage to Anne More do confirm his deep love for her, and many of Donne's greatest love poems reverberate with sincerity every bit as powerfully as his Divine Poems. But as we have noted before, the poems remain the final arbiters.

The Anniversarie is the final poem to endure close analysis in this chapter. Keeping in mind what has just been noted about sincerity combining with intellect, and form with feeling, read it before continuing with the detailed analysis.

The three-verse structure likens it to *Lovers Infinitenesse* but structural similarities are limited. As with *Lovers Infinitenesse*, some editions make each verse a single sentence, others place additional full stops at lines 12, 24 and 26. *The Anniversarie* is in rhyming couplets for the most part, with the final quatrain of each verse rhyming whereas *Lovers Infinitenesse* has a basic ababcdcd pattern, with the unusual addition that the last three lines of every verse use the same rhyme throughout – a subtle way of emphasising 'all'. The vital point is that both poems are extremely disciplined structurally, whatever our initial impression.

Donne begins *The Anniversarie* by placing the lovers firmly into the temporal, physical world while simultaneously implying their superiority. The high and mighty, 'Kings, and all their favourites', and 'honours, beauties, wits', even 'The Sun itself', may all be a year older now than when the lovers met, but they are immune to this ageing process:

> All other things to their destruction draw,
>   Only our love hath no decay;

(ll. 6–7)

This is typical hyperbole. It is quite a claim to outlive the sun, and we might recognise from the other items on the list something equally typical of Donne, his dislike of the court. Of all the things subject to decay and death he could have listed, he chose to limit this list to the courtly world, another reminder that he was writing within a very conventional tradition. Nevertheless, their love is placed outside time, and in a curious manner, although he admits its growth, it never changes, weakens or lessens, 'Running it never runs from us away'. The 'it' must refer to their love, but to describe love as 'running' is an odd and awkward image. Donne may be using it inferentially through its connection with time, where it belongs more comfortably. Time and love do indeed form the two halves of the entire dispute, so there is perhaps something wittily apt in this use of 'running'. The shift from 'it' to 'his' between lines 9 and 10 adds to the confusion. Extremely well read in theology, Donne would also have been aware of theological attempts to explain eternal life in terms of God's timelessness. However Donne perceived these few lines working, as they stand they assure us of the lovers' stability and fidelity. On this, their first anniversary, the prospect facing them is one of unshakeable love and unity.

The idea that they might be buried together allows him to express the depth of his love and claim that would mean they would never be separated, 'If one might, death were no divorce.' But the effects of time are not ultimately to be avoided, and he leaps to the future and their inevitable deaths, imagining them buried in two graves. It has been argued that this means the poem refers to an extra-marital affair, but if the speaker is unmarried, and this is hardly in question after one year, he would not presume to think of their burial in any other way if this poem is part of his courtship. Anything more would be ill-mannered and presumptuous.

Knowing that their bodies will decay, a truth Donne struggles with repeatedly in his poetry, he searches for a way of making their love survive death, and finds it by once more locating that love in their souls. Even 'Princes' die, he acknowledges, and using a familiar image of the lovers as royalty, as complete states unto themselves, he bemoans the loss of those physical attributes which have communicated their love, 'these eyes, and eares'. Yet this loss means little if, as he believes, their souls will continue to love each other in heaven, possibly even more intensely than on earth. The parenthesis '(All other thoughts being inmates)' might raise problems, but Donne is using 'inmates' to mean something foreign, or merely lodging there. Love is the only true occupant of the soul. Similarly a modern reader with little grounding in Christianity might not immediately appreciate the reference in line 20, 'When bodies to their graves, soules from their graves remove.' For Donne's readers this is simply a witty way of describing the Day of Judgement when it was believed all souls would return to their bodies before journeying to heaven or to hell. How this could actually happen was a question which engrossed some of the greatest theological minds, so it was hardly likely to escape Donne. Indeed it is a topic he was later to explore in his sermons.

The lines which begin the third verse have produced a little controversy. Clearly he looks forward to their being blessed with the reward of eternal life with God, but how he relates that to other souls, 'all the rest' concerns some writers. If we reread lines 21 to 24 as a unit, we can see Donne using simple repetition again, for emphasis, to guide the reader. The emphasis is on 'wee' and, if we read keeping that in mind, what we find is that he is saying that in heaven they will have no special status at all, but on earth they do. The weight falls on 'Here upon earth,' as opposed to in heaven. On earth they are 'Kings', in heaven they are like all other blessed souls, equal in God's presence. Pursuing their uniqueness, he logically reminds her that, as a state entire unto themselves, they are both subjects and kings. The image is not without its value or purpose because it then allows him to make the poem's strongest point. Complete unto themselves, no one can damage or harm them except themselves, and Donne assumes that is impossible in his tone and in the consistently stable, superior way he has described their love from the start:

> Who is so safe as wee? where none can doe
> Treason to us, except one of us two.

> (ll. 25–6)

He then exhorts them to ignore all kinds of dangers, whether true or false, and live and love 'nobly' until this first anniversary becomes their sixtieth. (Life expectancy being what it was in those days this is at least as good as saying forever.) 'Yeares and yeares unto yeares,' mimics longevity through its rhythm and makes an interesting contrast with line 6 of *Lovers Infinitenesse* where we saw Donne using the same technique to create a totally different mood. The relish with which he looks forward to this future is evident in the final phrase which he stresses with a caesura before 'this is the second of our raigne.' Whether 'only' is implied after 'is' or not in line 30, it is finally a gloriously optimistic, uplifting declaration of love and fidelity.

This analysis links *The Anniversarie* closely with *Lovers Infinitenesse*, both poems aching with sincerity and richly seductive. Is there a way in which we can separate these poems from others where seduction is a more blatant aim? Hopefully by this point we have carried out sufficient detailed analyses to see that there is the possibility that some of the *Songs and Sonnets* come from the pen of an older, wiser lover, a happily married man even. This may help to explain the unstable, shifting nature of some of his verse and the resulting annoyance of some of his critics. Similarly, in this chapter we have seen Donne bringing his considerable intellect to bear on notoriously difficult human dilemmas. How does love affect the individual? How do we manage rejection? What is a reasonable way to respond to undeserved hurt? How do we value love or ensure love lasts? How can we communicate those needs and desires most effectively? And one timely question in this study: How far now can Donne as a love poet be accused of selfishness, or egoism?

Donne delights in using his mind. Should we be surprised at all to see him engage it on some of the most fundamental human needs? If he fails to convey to us the beauty or personality of the woman he loves, perhaps this is because his experience had taught him there were more eloquent ways to seduce than to flatter. If, as we have surmised with a few of the poems, they were written for Anne More, it would be a dull mind indeed that failed to grasp that she must have been an exceptional woman. We need to be very confident of our perception of his intentions before we accuse him of failure at all. Even today, after a number of extremely acute literary minds have edited his work thoroughly, some of the *Songs and Sonnets* undoubtedly resist easy interpretation. By keeping in mind the close-knit readership these poems had at their conception, the fact that Donne was not writing in any sense to be widely read, that poetry was something he found hard to resist, we can resolve some of these difficulties. Writing is inherently a difficult task. Poetry especially so, and verse like Donne's, with its tight control of structure and immense wit is so difficult, it is absurd to imagine him completing it unless he was driven to. As his life and letters show, his ambition was always openly elsewhere, and so perhaps we should view his poetry primarily as his private struggle for understanding. It is a view which should gain even more credence when we come to read and analyse his religious poetry.

Suggested Work

- Read *The Canonization* and extract from it all the images which set the lovers above the common run of ordinary men. Then compare the poem with *Lovers Infinitenesse* and *The Anniversarie* closely. Do the three poems evoke three separate relationships or fail completely to differentiate? Finally, decide which poem is the most effective declaration of love.
- Read *The Triple Fool* and decide what Donne wants from his reader. How does he want them to think of him?

5

The Poet and Mortality

That death figures excessively in Donne's poetry is undeniable. No other English poet comes close in this respect. Even Thomas Hardy, whose vast poetic output is often criticised for its gloominess, exhibits nothing like Donne's fascination with death. His writing is permeated with images and ideas about death, and from his prose works and letters we know he suffered serious bouts of depression which led him to feel suicidal on occasions. In one letter to his friend Sir Henry Goodyer, he admits that suicide attracted him even when his prospects looked good and he was uninfluenced by tragic events. He wrote the first defence of suicide to be published in English, *Biathanatos*, and this passage from it gives us a taste of how seriously he regarded his own susceptibility. Referring to the attempted suicide of a contemporary theologian, Donne confesses:

> I have often such a sickely inclination. And whether it be, because I had my first breeding and conversation with men of a suppressed and afflicted Religion, accustomed to the despite of death, and hungry of imagin'd Martyrdome; Or that the common Enemie finde that doore worst locked against him in mee, Or that there be a perplexitie and flexibilitie in the docrine it selfe; Or because my Conscience ever assures me, that no rebellious grudging at Gods gifts, nor other sinfull concurrence accompanies these thoughts in me, or that a brave scorn, or that a faint cowardliness beget it, whensoever any affliction assailes me, mee thinkes I have the keyes of my prison in mine owne hand, and no remedy presents it selfe so soone to my heart, as mine own sword.[1]

Thankfully this was one remedy for depression he never actually tried, and, so fierce was the grip mortality had on his imagination, there could be worse ways of spending time in the company of other students than discussing how he would have gone about it. Students of Jacobean drama will probably find they have a head start. Interested readers might also wish to look into the way he prepared for his own death in 1631, which is well documented, and those fortunate enough to have geography on their side may even see how, by visiting St Paul's Cathedral today.

In this chapter we will be examining, as closely as ever, a number of poems where death figures prominently as part of Donne's poetic personality. We will try to find a way to accommodate them comfortably within his love poetry as a whole and to bring key biographical information into the analysis. As, it seems, with any great writer, Donne's life was hardly a straightforward business, yet how usefully we can employ our knowledge of it as an analytical tool is questionable. It has been the predominant approach of many critics, yet in his case there are severe difficulties created largely by the need for privacy when circulating manuscripts in the decidedly risky atmosphere of King James I's court. Time spent travelling abroad adds to this, and although there is material relating to his life, patrons and friends, as we have learned already, the heart of any analysis we make has to be the work itself. The sudden discovery of a previously unheard-of autobiography by Shakespeare might send publishers and academics into a feeding frenzy, but it would hardly alter the way we feel watching King Lear carrying the dead Cordelia in his arms, or Titania seducing an Ass.

We will begin with one of the most famous individual poems in the English language, *A Nocturnall upon S. Lucies Day*, and reserve wondering what gained it such an impressive reputation until our analysis is complete. Saint Lucy's Day for Donne was 13 December and although the Countess of Bedford's Christian name was Lucy, and he had a daughter of the same name, all that really matters for now is that it is the shortest day of the year. Now read the poem before commencing the analysis.

The poem opens with typical Donne compression. Not only is it the year's midnight, it is that single day's, and that day is Saint Lucy's

Day. The weight of darkness is emphasised further in the second line as he reminds us that 'scarce seaven houres' of day lighten the bleakness. That the sun itself is 'spent' we should find straightforward, but the use of 'flasks' and 'squibs' in lines 3 and 4 can lead to confusion. The type of flask Donne means is a powder horn, used for loading muskets, and a squib was a military word for a half-charge which was used in drill. It was believed that the stars stored sunlight, and so 'flasks' is acting as an image for them. In combination, what Donne wants us to picture is an entire universe dulled and dead, 'The world's whole sap is sunke.' We have encountered 'balme' earlier in our analysis of *The Extasie* in Chapter 3, but here it seems to have a looser meaning, although the image contained within line 6 is not wholly clear. The image becomes easier to cope with when we know how Donne is using 'hydroptique'. It is a word for dropsy, a disease which makes water accumulate in body tissue, but Donne uses it elsewhere to mean, by association, thirsty.

The subsequent image is also problematic but not because of vocabulary. Life itself has 'shrunke' to the 'beds-feet'. Perhaps the most consistent way to see this is that Donne is thinking of a flower bed because that is in keeping with 'sap', and the thirsty earth, which have preceded it. You may wish to see other potential meanings here, and if we find ourselves also thinking of a dead body, that is not surprising because the last line of the verse turns Donne himself into an Epitaph. Everything living he sees as shrivelled and dried up, 'Dead and enterr'd', yet so excessive is his sense of sorrow, all of these 'laugh' compared with him. By now we should be quick to recognise this as hyperbole.

It is something of an aside, but literature is a chain of overwhelming intricacy and exposing some of its links can never be a bad thing. Compare Donne's opening with these first two verses from Hardy's short poem, *The Darkling Thrush,* written on 31 December 1900:

> I leant upon a coppice gate
>   When frost was spectre-grey,
> And Winter's dregs made desolate
>   The weakening eye of day.

The tangled bine-stems scored the sky
    Like strings of broken lyres,
And all mankind that haunted nigh
    Had sought their household fires.

The land's sharp features seemed to be
    The Century's corpse outleant,
His crypt the cloudy canopy,
    The wind his death-lament.
The ancient pulse of germ and birth
    Was shrunken hard and dry,
And every spirit upon earth
    Seemed fervourless as I.

Donne's unremittingly grim opening as yet contains no mention
of the cause of all this misery. The reader waits in anticipation for a
hint, which comes with the first line of verse two when, by sug-
gesting would-be lovers should study him, he implies that love is
responsible. The rest of the second verse is reproduced below for us
to analyse in isolation before slotting it back into the poem as a
whole. It shows Donne at his most obtuse, and yet, paradoxically,
few students would say they do not appreciate the depth of misery
and sadness it evinces:

    For I am every dead thing,
        In whom love wrought new Alchemie.
        For his art did expresse
    A quintessence even from nothingnesse,
    From dull privations, and leane emptinesse
    He ruin'd mee, and I am re-begot
    Of absence, darknesse, death; things which are not.

(ll. 12–18)

If we think of 'Alchemie' as an unspecified chemical process, and
connect 'his art' (l. 14) and 'He' (l. 17) correctly with Love, personi-
fied in line 13, a workable interpretation of this passage is possible.
The 'Alchemie' is 'new' because Donne's misery is typically greater
than the misery Love normally creates. The 'dull privations, and
leane emptinesse' of line 16 conveys the dreadful sense of loss, of

absence he feels without the woman he loves. Having destroyed him, out of this vacuum of feeling Love manages to recreate him, from things incapable of fertility, 'absence, darknesse, death; things which are not.' In passages like this, Donne's use of hyperbole is so extreme it actually strains our ability to comprehend it as hyperbole. For something to strike us as exaggeration we need a realistic base from which to work, and on occasions Donne builds so toweringly, on so weak a foundation, we lose sight of the edifice itself. Yet it is precisely this hyperbole that gives the poem its great strength and makes it a favourite with some readers.

Verse three develops the same thought, almost as though Donne himself might have perceived the strain he was placing on his reader's comprehension. In comparison, he states, everyone else is capable of drawing nothing but good from everything they connect with. In them 'Life, soule, forme, spirit,' are fuelled by good. Only he is made, by Love's chemistry (a 'limbecke' is a piece of chemical apparatus), the burial place of everything negative. We were warned in chapter 1 to look out for paradox in Donne and here is as simple and clear an example as any, 'Of all, that's nothing.'

The echoing caesura after 'nothing', allows him a new thought and he reminisces for a moment about their past together and once more in quite astoundingly extreme terms. Their tears become Biblical floods in scale, drowning the entire world, which is possible because, as we have seen before, they were the entire world, 'us two'. Striving for even greater degree, Donne finds it by making them 'two Chaosses,' when they displayed any affection for things or people outside of their entire world of love. It is as though he reminds her of their mutual capacity to generate devastating jealousy. He then ends the verse with an image which resounds with echoes from poems we have analysed earlier. Absence from each other in the past sent their soules into withdrawal, leaving mere 'carcasses' behind. We will save a more detailed comparison of this image with sections from *A Valediction: forbidding mourning* and *A Feaver* for the Suggested Work section at the end of the chapter.

Over halfway through the poem we now appear to have the reason for this terrible show of grief. She is dead, and so this poem is in effect an elegy. Yet even the idea of her death seems to make no sense to him ('which word wrongs her'), and he persists in his deep-ening grief by claiming he has become something so utterly beyond compare in its emptiness, that his hyperbole once more evades us, it is so ingenious. We need some knowledge of Donne's theological reading to fully grasp the image in lines 28 to 29. The first nothing was conceived of by St Augustine, amongst others, as the idea of cre-ation in the mind of God before Creation took place. Donne describes himself as being made, by her death, the 'Elixer' or quin-tessence, of that first nothing. Is it surprising so many readers of Donne have found this poem an extraordinary articulation of loss? In his search for words which will convey the depth of his grief, Donne finds them in the baroque beauty of hyperbole and wit.

Insisting on this state of absolute blackness, he is able to form the darkly ironic supposition, 'Were I a man,' only to deny it forcefully and prefer to be 'any beast'. Even animals possess 'Some ends, some means' he believes, before insisting further that, 'Yea plants, yea stones' have emotions and can 'detest' and 'love'. Absolutely every-thing has some property, some quality which gives it meaning. Yet he is still no 'ordinary nothing' but the quintessence of the first nothing, just as 'shadow, a light, and body must be here.' It is worth while making sure we understand what links these three items here. Light and shadow are intangible, lacking substance, while the body Donne is thinking of lacks a soul and is therefore merely a shell, equally empty and useless.

This shatteringly bleak outlook persists into the final verse with the opening claim, 'But I am None'. If we look to link the 'None' closely we find it is difficult to pin it down to any of the possible objects in the preceding verse. Does Donne mean he is not 'an ordi-nary nothing' or a 'beast' or even further back into the verse, 'a man'? The latter has the strongest appeal since 'But I am None'; log-ically balances with 'Were I a man', in line 30. This explanation bears even more weight when the next clause comes into play, 'nor will my Sunne renew.' Brought to the very edge of life by his grief, Donne cannot imagine living beyond the nadir of this St Lucy's Eve. We might also think of his dead lover when he uses 'Sunne' since she is implicitly connected with darkness throughout the poem, a thought which helps us to a clearer understanding of the curious phrase 'the lesser Sunne' in line 38, which then becomes the sun itself. Donne's injunction to lovers to 'Enjoy your summer all', requires a little astrological knowledge to make good sense of it, although his use of 'Goat' is as much because it is a creature conventionally linked with lust as with the zodiacal sign of Capricorn. At this time of the year the sun does indeed enter the sign of Capricorn and reaches its farthest limit in the southern hemisphere. All of this is, however, merely for the benefit of others. Donne prepares himself for a different future. Picking up on the word 'enjoy' sardonically, he bitterly accepts the death of his lover, 'Since she enjoyes her long nights festivall', and readies himself to join her in death by renaming this day of the year hers, 'This houre her Vigill, and her Eve.'

The shape of the poem is beautifully rounded off in the final line where he takes us back to the opening and reminds us that this night is 'Both the yeares, and the dayes deep midnight.'

Now we can turn to arguments about who the poem was written for or about. Lucy, Countess of Bedford, lived at Twickenham Park from 1608 to 1618 and Grierson, Donne's first great editor, links it with *Twicknam Garden*. J.B. Leishman, in *The Monarch of Wit,* felt it was more likely to be about his wife, and noted how similar it was to *A Valediction: of Weeping*; other writers have toyed with various details within the poem itself to connect it with the Countess: most simplistically, the fact that both have Lucy in their titles! We should stick firmly to our principle that the work itself should be our primary source, and if we do this it is almost absurd to read the poem as adulterous, which is essentially what we have to do if it is not about Anne More. The depth of grief, the hopeless yearning for death, are not emotions borne out of the excitement, novelty, or simple lust of an extra-marital affair. What Donne conveys in *A Nocturnall upon S. Lucies Day* is the overwhelming sense of amputation which we feel under the strain of a loved one's death, the futility of continuing life without the companionship of someone so intimate and familiar they have become an essential part of our identity. What mistress has ever achieved so much, however drawn-out the affair?

In *A Valediction: of Weeping*, we find Donne once again mingling love and death. Read the complete poem below before the analysis which follows.

A Valediction: of Weeping

Let me powre forth
My teares before thy face, whil'st I stay here,
For thy face coines them, and thy stampe they beare,
And by this Mintage they are something worth,
    For thus they bee   5
    Pregnant of thee;
Fruits of much griefe they are, emblems of more,
When a teare falls, that thou falls which it bore,
So thou and I are nothing then, when on a divers shore.

On a round ball   10
A workeman that hath copies by, can lay
An Europe, Afrique, and an Asia,
And quickly make that, which was nothing, *All:*
    So doth each teare,
    Which thee doth weare,   15
A globe, yea world by that impression grow,
Till thy teares mixt with mine doe overflow
This world, by waters sent from thee, my heaven dissolved so.

O more than Moone,
Draw not up seas to drowne me in thy spheare,   20
Weepe me not dead, in thine armes, but forbeare
To teach the sea, what it may doe too soone;
    Let not the winde
    Example finde,
To doe me more harme, than it purposeth;   25
Since thou and I sigh one anothers breath,
Who e'r sighes most, is cruellest, and hastes the others death.

We have learned that a valediction is a farewell and need firstly to
assure ourselves we understand the situation which instigates these
lines. If we read them for clues to this we find the most useful in
lines 21 to 25, where Donne is anticipating a sea voyage. There he
urges his lover not to add to the dangers of wind and sea by her sighs
and tears. Like *A Valediction: forbidding mourning,* he is about to
journey abroad, and the anxiety this occasions for them both is the

theme of the poem. But the use of the preposition 'of' in the title is curiously unexpected and will need some further thought after the analysis.

So the poem begins with both the lovers tearfully anticipating his departure and Donne openly allowing the flow of tears. Why this flagrant display of sorrow is not stifled owes much to the conceit he develops from that point. 'For thy face coines them,' suggests that it is the sight of her weeping face which provokes his own, while 'and thy stampe they beare,' plays with the notion that her reflection is physically carried in the tears as they fall. But this only adds to their value, 'by this Mintage they are something worth,' and allows him to compliment her at the same time as displaying his own sorrow. The short lines and simple rhyming couplet then stress the conceit and invite the reader to respond to the starkly challenging image 'Pregnant of thee'. If we interrogate this compact image we find it rich in possibilities. The tears are pregnant as in swollen (the physical shape is being alluded to), but simultaneously they contain his lover's image, she is enveloped in each watery womb. Each is also the product of their love and therefore fertile. It is a fine example of how inventive and provocative Donne's poetic mind is, and the conceit has a long way to run before he exhausts it.

The result of 'much griefe', the tears are also emblematic of more to come, but the thought Donne then injects into the conceit may be less easy to see because of the unusual usage of 'that' in line 8. If we interrogate the phrase 'that thou' and remind ourselves of the core to the conceit, the reflection of her contained in each tear, we should be able to see that 'that' is an adjective describing 'thou', the subject of 'falls'. We have noted before that when a word is quickly repeated it is highly likely that Donne is punning, and here 'falls' refers not only to the physical dropping of the tears, but to his lover's demise. She is destroyed just as the image of her in each tear is destroyed, and, to maintain their unity in this whole process, he reminds us that he too endures this form of death, 'So thou and I are nothing then', and in the final few words places them conventionally on different shores, the result of his coming journey.

The whole verse accepts and bows to the inevitable grief occasioned by their parting, finding little comfort in the comparison of tears with coins, but instead binding them together as equal sufferers via the image of falling tears. The acknowledgement of this distress, the way Donne embraces it, signifies again that he is not dealing here with someone insignificant or of short-lived acquaintance. If this is a love poem, the object of it is no reluctant young virgin he is intent on seducing. He treats his lover here with immense intellectual as well as personal respect.

Donne continues to develop the conceit in the second verse using familiar words and ideas. Describing how a craftsman can make a globe by laying maps onto a formerly blank ball, he wittily highlights the paradox, 'And quickly make that, which was nothing, *All*'. But from there the conceit takes a difficult turn and editors' attempts to manage the difficulty by manipulating the punctuation do not really resolve it. If we examine our version above closely, in the way we have been practising in previous poems, we will be able to see the problem clearly, if not solve it. The 'So doth' is a very strong way of linking the two parts of this analogy, it leaves no room for ambiguity. The expectation is that we will understand something contained in the second part by reference to the image in the first. We need to keep the idea of *nothing quickly becoming all* then, in mind as we continue. Each tear of hers, almost a nothing in physical terms, becomes 'A globe, yea world.' In the same way that the craftsman created the globe by impressing maps upon it, her tears, multiplied, make an entire world. It is the familiar hyperbolic claim that the lovers' world is the world itself and nothing exists outside it. Mixed with his own tears, the combined weight of water (and grief) is enough to flood 'This world' and by implication, destroy it. It is line 18 which is especially awkward here, but however we might choose to arrange the punctuation, the sense that their combined tears are enough to dissolve Donne's 'heaven' is unavoidable.

One way to deal with this obstacle is to now go back and reread the whole poem up to the point where the meaning is uncertain. Frequently the reader finds his or her grasp of the awkward section is stronger, and the resistance loosened by holding the whole in mind, rather than persisting with a decoding approach. Often one meaning foregrounds itself in the process, sometimes even in an exhilarating way, and although it may not be the same meaning which strikes you at a later date, it is nonetheless valid for that. What we are aiming for is a coherent, aesthetic response to the poem rather than a set of cleverly argued, isolated explanations.

Contemporary fascination with astronomy comes into play again in verse three when Donne calls his lover 'O more than Moone,' and asks her not 'to drowne me in thy spheare'. Remembering the underlying image of tears as globes, spheres or worlds, he makes her greater than the moon because her power extends beyond the tides into other spheres. It is also unusual for a woman to be connected to the moon without raising the ghost of the goddess Diana and connotations of virginity. Calling her 'more than Moone,' then, may also confirm our view of this woman as a serious partner and not an object for seduction. She is certainly deeply enough in love with Donne to be in danger of weeping him to death. We may even choose to see an echo of his wife in 'more'. (Far more extravagant ideas have been imposed on Donne's poems on the basis of spectacularly less tenuous connections.) The phrase, 'Weepe me not dead' is intensely compact, implying both weeping because he is dead and killing him by her weeping. As noted already, the sea may do as much soon enough.

For the poem's final conceit, Donne turns away from tears to their associated sighs and reminds her not to teach the winds by her sighs to upset his sea journey any more than they have already decided to. It is an elegant, as well as logical step, from tears to sighs, but in the poem's final couplet Donne leaves us (and of course his lover) with even more to consider. The mingling of their mutual tears has been so intensely played upon throughout the poem, and the notion of them as separate beings so powerfully eroded, he can now claim they are incapable of separate breath, 'Since thou and I sigh one anothers breath', as though it were assumed. And since this is the case, whoever breathes most steals the other's breath, and by doing so brings them closer to death. It is undoubtedly worth while appreciating here again the poverty of the prose compared to the richness of Donne's poetry, 'Who e'r sighes most, is cruellest, and hastes the others death.' What he produces at the poem's end is a superbly logical and beautiful affirmation of his love. From a situation which trembles with grief and unites two people in an emotional dilemma, he creates a poignant love poem that not only confirms his love for her, but finds a way to combat the imminent threat to that love, the sea journey, by mutual courage.

Now we can return to our query about the title, *A Valediction: of Weeping*, and interrogate the 'of' in it. Is it a farewell to weeping, or a farewell: on weeping? If it was either Donne may well have written either. The variety of titles in the various manuscripts all prefer the 'of', even where 'tears' is substituted for 'weeping'. So we might be forgiven for concluding that the title as it stands is itself witty, and turns an uncertain poem 'on weeping' into a love poem, beautifully requesting an end to tears as a means to cope with separation.

Death and ideas associated with dying are widely used in Donne's verse and, from two poems where grief is a dominant emotion, we turn now to two poems where considering death gives rise to markedly different emotions, *The Funerall* and *The Dampe*. Read *The Funerall* first before the analysis.

The dramatic situation should be very clear. Donne imagines himself dead and about to be laid in his shroud. Even if we know little or nothing of the Catholic tradition of holy relics, we should recognise that the conceit centres on his having been given a love token by his lover, a 'subtile wreath of haire, which crowns my arme' (l. 3). As we know from the introduction, Donne was born into one of the most influential Catholic families in the country and received a fiercely Catholic education until he chose apostasy for himself. All of this at a time when persecution of Catholics was rife and horrific, and ignominiously public death a price commonly paid by priests or their protectors. Martyrdom offered an instant route to God, and therefore martyrs had a status akin to saints amongst the Catholic population, and their body parts were equally valued and honoured as holy relics. We can glean something of how great this status was today in the numerous reliquaries which are found in churches or museums all across Europe, containers built to hold the various body parts of saints or martyrs. The wealth of precious metals and jewels, as well as the immense artistry required in their construction, are evidence of how significant these relics really were to the Catholic mind. They truly were objects closer to God.

The Funerall could never have been conceived of, never mind written, by a Protestant mind, and this is true of *The Relique* too. Whatever faith Donne professed at the time of writing, and the warning in line 19 clearly voices Protestant scepticism, both poems owe their existence to a mind nurtured on heaven as its rightful home.

At his imagined death, then, Donne sees those about to shroud him hesitate and question the curious bracelet of hair about his arm and he begs them not to damage or consider it too deeply. Yet even more than the hair itself, it is what it represents he wants protected, 'The mystery, the signe you must not touch,' (l. 4). In his conceit, the token becomes his 'outward Soule', a stand-in for his true soul which has already gone to heaven at the moment of death but which leaves behind this substitute, 'Viceroy', to keep his body from 'dissolution' (l. 8).

Verse two is one of those lengthy sentences which can be very difficult to understand without finding a way to be sure of its structure. It is a method we have used before and bears repeating here because it is such a good example. The whole verse is reproduced below with the key connecting elements of the sentence highlighted to show the structure:

> **For if** the sinewie thread my braine lets fall
> Through every part,
> **Can tye** those parts, and make mee one of all;
> **These haires** which upward grew, and strength and art
> Have from a better braine,
> **Can better do'it**; Except she meant that I
> By this should know my pain,
> As prisoners then are manacled, when they're condemned to die.
>
> (ll. 9–16)

From the above we can see that Donne understands that the brain is the seat and source of the nervous system and from it all feeling and movement emanate, but further, that it is the core which combines the whole and can 'make mee one of all' (l. 11).

'These haires' are those making up the bracelet, and they 'upward grew,' not only in a physical sense, but in a spiritual one too. That the giver of the bracelet was set on higher things than Donne is evident from his assertion she had 'strength and art' 'from a better braine', and so is better able to 'do it': to bind him as one being and prevent the dissolution feared in verse one. His hope is that her gift of the bracelet of her hair was intended to protect and perhaps even revitalise him after death until the caesura after 'do'it;' (l. 14) introduces the harsh note of doubt around 'Except', where the closest modern equivalent would be 'unless'. That 'unless' is quickly pursued to arrive at a contrasting explanation for the gift. Perhaps, Donne thinks, it was given to remind him of the pain she caused him, just as prisoners condemned to die are handcuffed. The poet has become as uncertain as those about to inter him, and like the reader seeks a better explanation.

Yet 'What ere shee meant by'it, bury it with me,' he orders, and, in providing the reasons why, resolves the riddle and makes the poem complete. Continuing the Catholic imagery, by describing himself as 'Loves martyr,' he makes it clear his love for her was unrequited and her neglect has been the cause of his death. We are in familiar territory. To avoid any accusations of Catholic sympathies he makes sure the existence of the bracelet around his arm is not misunderstood and so 'might breed idolatrie,' by becoming a holy relic. The sense of the last quatrain relies on a familiar pattern, 'As 'twas' . . . *x* . . . 'So, 'tis' . . . *y* . . . and in this link lies the force of the poem and its success. Just as in verse one it was humility which led Donne to ascribe to her love token the powers of a soul, which he did when making it the soul's 'Viceroy': now it is bravado which allows him to remind her of her neglect and bury her token with his own corpse. The implication in 'since you would save none of mee,' (l.24), is that she has rejected his advances in the time-honoured way of poetically reluctant virgins and his revenge, petty though it is, is to bury her with him as well as he can, and if that means only her gift of a wreath of her hair, it is no less a victory.

But if this were all, the poem would have little of the force and wit I have suggested above. As with so many of Donne's love poems it is crucial we see them as texts to be read by a lover, imaginary or not. When we adopt this tactic, ambiguities otherwise hidden become glaring, and here they revolve around 'So, 'tis some bravery', (l. 23). Bravado is fake, empty of real courage; Donne realises this, and so beneath this outward show of bitterness lies the possibility of still unquenched desire. It is as though he knows the whole poem is a charade, a failed attempt to break her hold over him. How we imagine any woman would respond to this, is again a question most usefully left for discussion.

The poem for us to consider in conjunction with *The Funerall* is *The Dampe*. It is reproduced below.

The Dampe

When I am dead, and Doctors know not why,
    And my friends curiositie
Will have me cut up to survay each part,
When they shall finde your Picture in my heart,
    You thinke a sodaine dampe of love   5
    Will through all their senses move,
And worke on them as mee, and so preferre
Your murder, to the name of Massacre.

Poore victories! But if you dare be brave,
    And pleasure in your conquest have,   10
First kill th'enormous Gyant your *Disdaine*,
And let th'enchantresse *Honor*, next be slaine,
    And like a Goth and Vandall rize,
    Deface Records, and Histories
Of your owne arts and triumphs over men,   15
And without such advantage kill me then.

For I could muster up as well as you
    My Gyants, and my Witches too,
Which are vast *Constancy*, and *Secretnesse*,
But these I neyther looke for, nor professe;   20
    Kill me as Woman, let mee die
As a meere man; doe you but try

Your passive valor, and you shall finde then,
Naked you'have odds enough of any man.

The title of the poem presents us with our first problem because the meaning of 'damp' today is most commonly linked simply to moisture, whether as an adjective or, less commonly, a noun. For Donne's age, and he survived one of the worst of the great plagues to decimate London, by moving out to Chelsea, the word carries far greater fear and weight. We need to appreciate that it was used to describe a noxious vapour of some kind, as in fire-damp or choke-damp, the gas feared by all miners. In Donne's poem, it is clearly imagined as something immediately potent, 'Will through all their senses move' (l. 6), and fatal, 'And worke on them as mee' (l. 7). His vivid imagination reduces the entire surgical crew he has participating in his autopsy to a mound of corpses courtesy of his mistress's poisonous picture in his heart.

That Donne begins this poem not with his own imagined death, but even more curiously with an autopsy, is further evidence of his intense concern with his own mortality and the fate of his soul. It is a common and weak fantasy of the spurned lover, to imagine their own death and the consequent grief of their ex-lover, but Donne characteristically strides ahead to imagine a scene of absolute carnage worth the name of 'Massacre'.

The opening situation is typically challenging. Donne, a presumably young and healthy man, is dead. So unexpected is this that his friends insist on an autopsy to discover the reason. To imagine his own death is hardly a comforting activity, but to picture himself displayed like a cadaver in some anatomy lesson is even more bizarre, and yet the tone cleverly avoids anything distasteful or ugly. The first verse's fluent, single sentence succeeds because it appears that he is addressing the mistress. The intimate use of 'You' and 'your' in lines 5 and 8, undermines our ability to feel repelled because it simultaneously acknowledges the fantasy. Donne is not dead, she could not possibly kill him out of neglect, and they are both fully aware that he is using hyperbole for effect. By now we should be able to recognise the voice of seduction, even in the heart of such a grim dramatic situation. It is such a gross exaggeration to call your mistress a murderess solely because she deserts you or declines to sleep with you, that the convention itself is almost humorous, but to blame her for a massacre is something else entirely. That is an impressive compliment.

But the tone of the sensitive, hurt lover continues with the cry, 'Poor victories!' which begins verse two. The caesura then gives the reader pause for thought before Donne issues a greater challenge which is couched entirely in gender terms. 'But if you dare be brave' (l. 9) is followed by a list of escapades linked by their essentially masculine nature. The chivalrous slayer of personified giants and enchantresses is obviously a male figure, and both the Goths and Vandals are used by Donne here, not only because of their historical reputation for barbarism, defacing records and history, but for their cruelty. Why would Donne address his mistress in these very male terms? In the world of Jacobean England the idea has far greater resonance than today where images of women carrying weapons into various conflicts has been a shocking reality since the Eastern front of the Second World War. To what extent is this essentially male challenge a compliment? 'Of your own arts and triumphs over men' (l. 15) acknowledges her social experience, while the continued use of the idea of dying for love possibly hints at her sexual experience. Donne's invitation to 'kill me then' therefore, is possibly far bolder and intimate than we might first believe.

If we appreciate his witty use of their gender differences here, then we can see that the poem is yet again one of seduction; a love poem hidden discreetly beneath a funeral shroud to make it all the more enticing. After all, he only issues the challenges at all on the condition that she 'dare be brave', and 'pleasure' in her 'conquest' (ll. 9–10). He is nothing if not confident about his own ability to provide that pleasure.

But we should not bypass the two key figures chosen to represent her monsters in verse two. Using personification in a way made most familiar in John Bunyan's Christian allegory, *Pilgrim's Progress*, Donne cites '*Disdaine*' and '*Honor*' as the chief barriers to their joy. The latter is clearly intended to undermine her decision to deny him sex in a way we have seen already in poems like *The Flea*. Honour is an illusion, a deceit, and, by association here with magic, almost a

sin. Disdain is a far more interesting choice and repays considera-
tion. For Donne's age the word came hand in hand with superiority.
One only felt disdain for one's inferiors. As a Catholic, and depen-
dent on employment for an income, Donne was probably inferior to
most of the young ladies he met at court or during his twenties, but
the temptation to tie this in with the known facts about his clandes-
tine relationship with Anne More is there. One word may seem
slender evidence for the idea, but, as we have seen elsewhere, a close
and thoughtful consideration of the entire poem, divorced from
external biographical or chronological evidence of various kinds, is
often the most fruitful analysis.

Verse three begins in a way we might recognise from work done
in Chapter 4 on *Womans Constancy*, and a close comparison of the
two poems is a very useful exercise. For the moment it is enough just
to recognise the same tone built upon his use of the same plaintive
words, 'for' and 'could', equally implying a sense of sad yet proud
resignation. Donne's 'Gyants' and 'Witches' differ in a fascinating
way from his mistress's. His are '*Constancy*' and '*Secretnesse*', and his
denying that he either looks for them in her, or professes them
himself, is actually no denial at all; he deliberately juxtaposes them
with her '*Honor*' and '*Disdaine*' to make her monstrous champions
look decidedly shabby. The emphatic pause at the end of line 20
allows the amorous poet space to prepare for his truly elegant *coup de
grace*. But the lines here may resist our comprehension because of
Donne's compact use of simple language to create the antithesis:

> Kill mee as Woman, let mee die
> As a meere man;'

(ll. 21–2)

It is the conventional Jacobean toying with death and orgasm we
have noted in earlier analyses, a passionate pleading to be loved by
her in the only way every heterosexual young man believes counts.
Chasing away the brave claims and ethical barriers to their love, he
wants her and her only. And to sugar the pill to perfection Donne
ends with a potent and beautifully timed compliment which does far
more than play on her feminine vanity:

> doe you but try
> Your passive valor, and you shall finde then,
> Naked you'have odds enough of any man.
>
> (ll. 22–4)

Naked, she is lovely enough to defeat any man, but it is the witty oxymoron, 'passive valor', and the deeply provocative image of her it creates, which would appeal most to any girl of intelligence.

From a morbid, unpromising beginning, where Donne sees his corpse opened out in the most grotesque manner, he gently slides into a love poem of remarkably seductive quality. Death is transformed into something fertile and delicious, and a poem which initially appears to attack and undermine his mistress, ends up in supreme awe of her. And there is one more teasing thought arising from our earlier speculation about Anne More. How did he know, 'Naked' she had 'odds enough of any man'?

We can now gather together what this chapter has added to our developing appreciation of Donne, and form some conclusions. It has shown that death is a favourite theme of Donne's, yet one absolutely at the mercy of his poetic will. We are as likely to encounter it in an erotic context as a funereal one.

Donne's Catholicism frequently tints his imagery of death and the grave, and may, in some instances, help us to understand the otherwise bizarre nature of some of his reflections on corpses and graves. We have examined Donne's poetic expression of grief in some detail and attempted to suggest there may be biographical reasons for this.

Finally, it should be noted here that as we turn from the love poetry to the divine, this crucial aspect of his work will become even more significant, perhaps merely mirroring what it did for him in reality.

Suggested Work

• Compare the way Donne conveys grief in *A Nocturnall upon St Lucies Day* with *A Feaver* and *A Valediction: forbidding mourning*.

- Read and do a close analysis of *The Expiration* with the aim of deciding how it uses death.

- Read *Loves Deitie* and pay particular attention to the effects of the final couplet.

- Read and do a close analysis of *The Relique* before finding further information about its possible biographical significance.

6

From Secular to Divine

Donne's poetry has, in the past, been the object of censorious editors and critics. The simple truth that he wrote a large number of poems dedicated to the worldly experience of men pursuing women, yet as many entirely set on the divine, has frustrated and annoyed many earlier readers who frequently ignored one or the other in their confusion. We live in a less censorious age, but the dichotomy is one the twentieth century has been every bit as eager to demolish. It is not hard for us, in our post-Freudwinian heaven, to see that a man can write about love and God, and indeed seek both. Yet the tradition still persists that, in some odd way, the John Donne who wrote the love poetry had to become a different, chastened individual for him to write the divine poetry. His ordination is already neatly in place to act as the perfect explanation, as though after it he somehow became, not only obsessed with eschatological thought (concern for the fate of one's soul) but celibate into the bargain.

Anne died over three years after his ordination, after giving stillbirth to another child. Yet examiners persist in asking questions which assume this secular–divine division. It is sensible, therefore, that in this chapter we examine those poems which will enable us to explore this dichotomy and understand it more sensitively. From the start we can use what has been learned about Donne's early life, education and upbringing to undermine the tempting picture of a married man traversing middle age and abandoning his worship of women for worship of God. It is the product of an unholy alliance between comments from Walton's *Life* and twentieth-century cultural practices and literature. Donne was given a thorough education by Jesuits, at a time when your faith could determine whether you even reached middle age or not, and religious thought is engrained not only in his head but in his work from a very early period. The first of the poems for analysis demonstrates this very clearly. *Satyre* III, 'On Religion', can be dated to roughly 1595 when Donne was 21, and belongs as we have learned with the other satires, to Donne's period at Lincoln's Inn. Read it before the analysis which follows.

Reading *Satyre* III may have proved something of a challenge if this comment of Coleridge's is to be believed. 'If you would teach a scholar in the highest form how to read, take Donne, and of Donne this satire.'[1] Our first question stems directly from this. What did Coleridge hear in the poem which gave rise to such a claim? It may help if we finish the quotation. 'When he has learnt to read Donne, with all the force and meaning which are involved in the words, then send him to Milton, and he will stalk on like a master, *enjoying* his walk.' Coleridge's italics are the key. Clearly by reading he meant something far more than the mere processing of the words and syntax. For Coleridge reading poetry is a vital, enlivening experience, richly stimulating but inherently difficult. It should not be a chore but a delight, something to be enjoyed. And that pleasure can only come out of an intimate, informed and alert response to the rhythms and structures of the poem, and to the ideas that nexus of artistry conveys. In Donne's *Satyre* III he found a rich combination of sound and feeling, thought and structure. What we should have grasped in our own reading is precisely 'all the force and meaning' in the words. An awareness of the techniques and effects which contribute to that is one of the key skills this study aims to teach, and hopefully work done in earlier chapters has already made the initial reading of *Satyre* III far less problematic than it might have been.

If we read the opening four lines again, aloud, aiming to convey the feeling, we should be able to see immediately why Coleridge was attracted to the poem. The harsh consonants of the first line, 'Kinde', 'chokes' and 'scorn', and the abrupt caesura after 'spleene' before the poem has even begun, are all indicative of anger. The poet's frustration depicts him able neither to cry nor laugh, yet intensely troubled. If the use of 'spleene' is difficult, we need to know that in Donne's time it was the source of both humour and sorrow. We still use the adjective 'splenetic' but medical science has somewhat outstripped the language. Donne acknowledges his own anger in the 'railing' of line 4 before introducing the poem's theme more calmly:

> Is not our Mistresse faire Religion,
> As worthy of all our Soules devotion,
> As vertue was to the first blinded age?
>
> (ll. 5–7)

We learned in Chapter 1 that religious imagery peppers his love poetry and should we therefore be surprised to see here how easily he adopts a sexual image to describe a religious quest? Playing on the convention of men worshipping their lovers with their souls, something he himself does repeatedly, he makes the search for religious truth a 'Mistresse' without the slightest hesitation. To understand the rest of the image and the way he develops it, we need to recognise that for Donne 'the first blinded age' is the classical world before Christianity. It seems to baffle him to think that ancient philosophers might confront his own father in heaven with their own beliefs equally accounted as faith, and be able to witness his own soul damned in spite of his father's caring instruction. The outrage in his tone is marked by another caesura in line 15 after 'damn'd' and the emotional injunction:

> O if thou dar'st, feare this;
> This feare great courage, and high valour is.
>
> (ll. 15–16)

where the 'feare this/ This feare' repetition is a witty, emphatic, spiritual call to arms or challenge. It is worthwhile asking here, who is being challenged? The paradox drives home the point as well as the full stop which ends what has been an almost breathless tirade. If we reread the first 15 lines and accentuate the rhyme, we can see also how firmly rhyme is subordinate to sense. Although entirely in rhyming couplets, we almost fail to notice them because his frequent enjambement (ll. 1–2, 8–9, 10–15) disguises them so effectively.

Having drawn our attention to the issue, the search for religious truth, he now embarks on a lengthy series of rhetorical questions which you should isolate and analyse one at a time until the caesura in line 28 after 'words?' Knowing that salamanders were supposedly cold-blooded and fire-proof, and that the 'Children in the oven' refers to the biblical story of Shadrach, Meshach and Abednego, should be sufficient extraneous knowledge for most readers. Together, the questions illustrate earthly acts of courage or daring which Donne sets up merely to topple with the dismissively brief, 'Courage of straw!' (l. 28). He is far more concerned to locate and acclaim true courage, which he does by continuing the same belligerent metaphor:

> O desperate coward, wilt thy seeme bold, and
> To thy foes and his (who made thee to stand
> Sentinell in his worlds garrison) thus yeeld,
> And for the forbidden warres, leave th'appointed field?
>
> (ll. 28–31)

God has made us and placed us on earth to partake in the only battle. All other conflicts are irrelevant when the true foe is known, and Donne employs rhythm again to signal the significance of the idea. 'Know thy foes', he proclaims, curtly, before 'The foule Devill' makes his appearance.

Donne uses the second person throughout the poem and, although we have already raised the question of who the poem really addresses, we have not answered it, since the answer is not simple. The poem opens firmly in the first person and only a sudden shift in line 11, 'shall thy fathers spirit' disturbs that. However, as we read on, it is noticeable that the use of the second person does not diminish the emotion, or the passion; the tone does not shift into one of distanced address, and so we can assume that, however relevant we might view the questions, they are primarily a matter of intense concern for Donne. He is disputing primarily with himself. This raises some interesting questions for writers eager to use Donne's life to analyse his verse, since the list of daring actions might well refer to his own youthful exploits. (He certainly fought against Spain as we know.)

The lengthy, complex sentence from line 33 to line 42 provides us with a good opportunity to put into practice a technique we have already learned. Analyse it as a single sentence by locating the key words which help you to grasp its structure. The use of 'last,' in line 39 is an example and it may also help to appreciate his image of the world as a tired whore, by knowing that, in Donne's era, the notion that the world was likely to end soon was a common one amongst theologians.

Hopefully we have appreciated the central idea. Donne rails at himself (and us) for being preoccupied with earthly things at the expense of his eternal soul. You may also have noted at the end of the sentence how he again sees the body as the tool by which the soul experiences the world, an idea explored in some detail in *The Extasie*. Using the close relationship between rhythm and meaning we have been alerted to, we should immediately be aware of the significance of the caesura in line 43 which turns 'Seek true religion', into a forceful statement of intent. It is in effect the central idea of the entire satire, and the perplexity it gives rise to is instantly captured by the rhetorical, 'O where?' The answer is delayed by a lengthy sequence of possible examples from line 39 to 69 which should not deter us because of the conventional use of classical names for imaginary fellow seekers after truth. Again we can use our growing experience of reading Donne to analyse what may at first appear a daunting passage. Always in command of structure, for each of the five names mentioned, Donne pursues the same pattern and, by analysing the first in detail, we can more easily deal with the others. Mirreus, believing religion dead in England, keeps faith with Roman Catholicism merely because of its ancient link with Christianity. This, Donne believes, is like contemporaries who pay as great a homage to the cloth which adorns the throne as the Prince himself. That brings us to the sentence end at line 48. The same structure is then used for each, so that their particular belief is described, then castigated via an analogy which exposes their shallow thinking. Now carry out the same analysis on the remaining names, which all fit neatly into one sentence, except for Graccus, the last, whose analagous weakness ends with the phrase, 'too much light breeds' (l. 69). It may be necessary to know that 'values' (l. 62) refers both to the idea of paying a fine for breaking a wedding engagement and for not attending Anglican services if you were a Catholic.

We should have formed a clear understanding of the passage now, as well as appreciated just how tightly Donne shapes his verse. Even this relatively early poem, full of emotion and passion as it is, is firmly under control: something Coleridge would have admired enormously.

The next section of the poem is the most important and has implications for students of Donne that go way beyond the poem itself. At the time of writing, Donne was undergoing a crisis of faith himself, desperately trying to resolve the clash between his ambitions and his inherited faith. As a scholar and intellectual, frequenting aristocratic circles, he was eager for a position of influence and power, but as a Catholic these were firmly denied him. Exactly when he abandoned the religion of his birth and became an Anglican we need not consider, but when he was appointed to the kind of post he yearned for, secretary to Sir Thomas Egerton in 1597, aged 25, he must certainly have been already accepted as such. In 1610 he published a prose work called *Pseudo-Martyr*, a ferociously anti-Jesuit piece undoubtedly designed to win him further favour amongst the authorities and at court. In *Satyre* III, then, it seems sensible to agree with John Carey when he calls it, 'the great, crucial poem of Donne's early manhood',[2] because it so clearly deals with his intellectual struggle during this critical period of his life.

Our analysis so far has brought to light some aspects of that crisis: his emotional turmoil, the firm grasp he had of contemporary religious controversy, his youthful energy and greed for glory, but it is the next section of the poem which is the most articulate and evocative. Dismissing the liberal-minded Graccus, in a short passage which slides more definitely towards the second-person form of address than any other, he urges that we spare no energy or resource in seeking truth. His injunction that we 'ask thy father' is especially poignant when we recall that his natural father died when he was three, and the fate of his soul must have perturbed Donne immensely during this spiritual crisis. 'Hee's not of none, nor worst, that seekes the best' (l. 75), Donne states, with considerable tolerance, adding wisely an idea his Catholic upbringing would ironically have driven home:

To stand inquiring right, is not to stray;
To sleepe, or runne wrong is.

(ll. 78–9)

Not surprisingly, Donne finds an answer to the perplexity which has dogged the poem from its clamorous opening in a poetic image, and again a caesura marks this significant image off from the argument that has led to it:

On a huge hill,
Cragged, and steep, Truth stands, and hee that will
Reach her, about must, and about must goe;
And what the hills suddennes resists, winne so;
Yet strive so, that before age, deaths twilight,
Thy Soule rest, for none can worke in that night.

(ll. 79–84)

Using arduous rhythm in line 81 to match the labour of the task, he sees that task as an entirely intellectual one. Truth is there for those set on seeking her, but, like an immensely difficult mountain, is accessible only to the most determined and courageous. And to remind us of his previous assertion that such a journey is the only one worth taking, he wishes us success, before death overtakes us and denies us the means to travel. The urgency and immense importance he gives the task is further underscored in the next concise line where the weight of the rhythm falls heavily on the final command, 'To will implyes delay, therefore now doe'.

The compact, elliptical expression which follows should be less resistant now if we have assimilated the analytical techniques from chapter to chapter. If we look for the missing words, or where words are working in more than one way, we should be able to see that 'too' provides the key. Just as difficult deeds require physical exertion, difficult knowledge requires great mental exertion. Donne is using the verb 'reach,' directly with 'The minde's indeavours', but is forcing it to work by association with the previous phrase about pain and the body. It is the kind of economic, compressed use of language which baffles many readers but it is also quintessentially poetic. Poetry often proceeds not so much by what it directly states, as what it elides: which is why Coleridge can view it as an active, vital experience for the reader. The next image is far less obtuse, although knowing that for Catholics the word 'mysteries' has a very particular meaning adds greatly to our appreciation of it. A religious mystery, for Donne, was something so intimately connected with God that it was unknowable by mankind. Some of the faith's most troubling questions were comfortably side-stepped by Catholic theologians via the simple solution of nominating them mysteries. What we should appreciate is that at this point in the poem Donne clearly dismisses anything unknowable. If at any moment in this satire we can hear his youthful mind warring with the faith of his birth, it is here.

The final movement of the poem is oddly, in a sense, away from religion to politics, perhaps because it so dominated the other half of his world at the time. He maintains his hold on the central drive towards truth, but sets it against a world of men, kings and power itself. Urging us to keep a firm hold on the truth we have found for ourselves, he asserts that God is not so dreadful that he has empowered kings to kill as they please. And if we are puzzled by the line, 'Nor are they Vicars, but hangmen to Fate' (l. 92), we need only to assign the pronoun 'they' thoughtfully. If we do, the resulting sense might explain why Donne in a later letter expressed some anxiety about his *Satyres* being widely read. We will see in the later section, on critical studies, that some writers have attributed a lot of Donne's intensity and passion to a widely felt Protestant despair. A stultifyingly sense of depression arising from the Calvinistic notion that God has not only already decided who is to be saved and who damned, but that there is nothing at all the individual soul can do on earth to prevent it. That Donne was far from that state of mind when writing *Satyre* III is self-evident when we consider the image of God he gives us in it.

Rekindling the emotion by calling himself (and us) 'Foole and wretch,' he reminds us that man's laws are meaningless on the Day of Judgement, and binds the poem firmly into the religious controversy of his age by listing a number of names we all probably need help with. In order they are: Philip II of Spain, Pope Gregory XIII or possibly the XIV, Henry VIII and lastly Martin Luther, their connection being that claiming them as fathers of your faith on the last day will gain you nothing. If we are tempted now to move quickly on, we ought to at least see that, as representatives of the two conflicting Christian beliefs of his age, it is interesting to see how he rejects them both equally; more evidence to add to our view of this poem as one born out of the crisis of his faith, rather than its resolution.

Advising us to understand rightly the bounds of power, and he has already located them in heaven and not on earth, he uses an image which is curiously earthbound to conclude the poem. The image, 'As streames are, Power is', runs from line 103 to the end of the poem. Analyse it closely now and see where you might find it inconsistent or lacking. You might wish to consider how flowers function in the image. However we respond to this final section of the poem, its conclusion is clear and consistent with the satire's central drive and intellectual concern:

> So perish Soules, which more chuse mens unjust
> Power from God claym'd, than God himselfe to trust.

(ll. 109–10)

We should recall here that satire was viewed as a potentially dangerous form, and reflect on the challenge to kingly authority the poem embodies. Donne's grandmother was a niece of Sir Thomas More, a relative Donne was proud to claim. Ironically (in view of Donne's imminent apostasy), who better to exemplify the ideal Donne seeks in the final couplet of his poem, than the one man whose principled stand against Henry VIII's dispute with Rome cost him his life.

Before embarking on analyses of some of Donne's *Holy Sonnets*, we will examine two nominally secular poems. *Twicknam Garden* is the first of these. It is a particularly useful poem to attempt at this point because most of the potentially difficult images it employs we have met already, and it proceeds in an extremely logical, clear manner. In some respects it is a wholly typical Donne poem. Even the shape of it on the page declares how beautifully structured it is, and yet it employs rhyme and rhythm almost entirely to suit the sense. The images are fascinatingly hyperbolic and inventive, and the ending typically surprising, paradoxical and puzzling. Read it through, trying hard to follow the argument as Donne develops it, and noting any usage of religious images. It has been reproduced completely below before an analysis which concentrates on this question of how Donne employs religious imagery in secular poems.

Twicknam Garden

Blasted with sighs, and surrounded with teares,
    Hither I come to seeke the spring,
    But at mine eyes, and at mine eares,
Receive such balmes, as else cure everything;
    But O, selfe traytor, I do bring   5
The spider love, which transubstantiates all,
    And can convert Manna to gall,
And that this place may thoroughly be thought
    True Paradise, I have the serpent bought.

'Twere wholesomer for mee, that winter did   10
    Benight the glory of this place,
    And that a grave frost did forbid
These trees to laugh, and mocke mee to my face;
    But that I may not this disgrace
Indure, nor yet leave loving, Love let mee   15
    Some senslesse peece of this place bee;
Make me a mandrake, so I may groan here,
    Or a stone fountaine weeping out my yeare.

Hither with christall vyals, lovers come,
    And take my teares, which are loves wine,   20
    And try your mistresse Teares at home,
For all are false, that tast not just like mine;
    Alas, hearts do not in eyes shine,
Nor can you more judge womans thoughts by teares,
    Than by her shadow, what she weares.   25
O perverse sexe, where none is true but shee,
    Who's therefore true, because her truth kills mee.

If we completed the reading with a decent understanding of the little narrative it contains, but are confused by the conclusion, we should not be surprised or disappointed. *Twicknam Garden* is absolutely typical of Donne in its contradictions and inconsistencies, which insist on provoking the reader. Donne's poems, as we have intimated repeatedly, are not riddles to be solved, but invitations to think.

He begins this one imagining himself entering a beautiful garden in the spring, indeed seeking the spring because he is 'Blasted with sighs, and surrounded with teares,' the conventional spurned lover. Elizabethan gardens were models of order and harmony, and in this one Donne finds all the ease created by flowers and birds he would wish, 'such balmes, as else cure every thing' (l. 4), until he destroys it himself by bringing with him 'The spider love, which transubstanti-ates all'. If we are troubled by his choice of 'spider', it is the popular misconception of them as venomous which he is using.

More pertinent, given our instruction, is the wonderfully incon-gruous 'transubstantiantes', surely one of the most unwieldy words in the language and yet one which Donne slides effortlessly into the rhythm. Why? An answer will emerge as our analysis continues, but for the moment we need to appreciate its theological meaning, the one Donne would have immediately comprehended as a Catholic. It refers to the conversion of the bread and wine of the holy sacrament into the body and blood of Christ. It is perhaps the word at the very core of the Reformation, the idea which fuelled Protestantism. Catholics believe that at the moment of communion, in some myste-rious way, the communion host and wine are changed into the flesh and blood of their saviour. This was a flight of fancy too far for the ascetic minds of the great Protestant reformers, and for a Protestant the communion remains only a symbolic act of remembrance.

Donne's use of it here immediately transforms the poem. What could be a slight and even vain excursion into self-pity, goes off the scale in significance. The grandeur of the situation becomes clearer in the final couplet of the first verse where he turns the undoubtedly beautiful, but nonetheless humble, *Twicknam Garden* into Eden:

> And that this place may thoroughly be thought
> True Paradise, I have the serpent bought.

(ll. 8–9)

In the second verse, as he wishes it were winter so that the garden's dead and dismal appearance was more in keeping with his own lovelorn mood, religious overtones creep in again in the phrase, 'and mocke mee to my face', which echoes Christ's taunting before the Crucifixion. It would be difficult for many of Donne's contemporaries to have got this far without also thinking of the Garden of Gethsemane and the night of self-examination Christ undergoes there before his arrest.

Overcome by the misery of his unrequited love, Donne asks the personified Love to transform him into either a mandrake or a fountain, the former groaning in pain, the latter weeping. It is the latter which has most appeal. Imagining himself a fountain, he pictures lovers coming to gather his tears in 'christall vyals,' which they take home to compare in taste with their mistresses'. Of course, 'all are false, that tast not just like' Donne's. The spelling of 'christall' (though Donne's usual one) and the notion of tears as 'loves wine', bind the whole intellectual level of the poem back into the religious, originally instigated by his brazen use of 'transubstantiates'. The sacrament of communion and the enormous weight it carries as an act of faith and devotion, bolsters what might otherwise be viewed as a selfish, rather whining little complaint. But as so often the case, Donne saves his most provocative thinking for the end.

In contrast with the elaborate imagery which has preceded it, the concluding reflections are couched in simple language, undemanding and plaintive. 'Alas, hearts do not in eyes shine,' he states sadly, and it is as impossible to know a woman's thoughts from her tears, as to describe her garments by observing her shadow. The voice of the rejected lover seems pathetically to triumph. Donne appears to resort to misogyny in the final couplet, until the consciously riddling nature of the words once more brings us up against our own incomprehension and demands we think for ourselves:

> O perverse sexe, where none is true but shee,
> Who's therefore true, because her truth kills mee.

(ll. 26–7)

A strong shift in expectation is something we have encountered before, and if that is what we have here, we might be prompted to see the poet finally accepting his lover's rejection of him, sadly yet kindly acknowledging her honesty. Perhaps he even loves her the more for it since she is clearly the only one of her sex whom he believes is 'true'. We may choose instead to find something shockingly sexual in his abrupt use of 'kills', or may settle for the view of the rejected lover persisting in his rejection to the point of death. However we respond, if we think about the words and their complex relationship to what has gone before, we have been the reader Coleridge approves of, and Donne would have wanted.

We should not leave *Twicknam Garden* without noting that it is one of the few poems for which we have some evidence of its composition. Inconclusive though that evidence is, it is possible that the poem was written for Lucy, the Countess of Bedford, when Donne was wooing her as a patron. The Countess was a keen patron of the arts and considered herself something of an intellectual, and bought the house at Twickenham in 1607, when Donne was 35. We do not know whether or not she ever even saw the poem, though we do know Donne flattered her considerably in his letters in search of financial support, and he was often a guest at her house. Whatever the truth about its composition, *Twicknam Garden* survives to speak for itself.

There is one more poem to consider before we can begin analysing poems we can unqualifyingly locate in the divine section of the Donne canon. Donne wrote a number of poems for rich patrons and friends, which was a perfectly normal practice for someone in his position at the time. He was in fact very quick to seek advantage when it could be found through his poetry, as the astonishingly fulsome *Anniversaries* , written after the death of Sir Robert Drury's daughter, Elizabeth, demonstrate. Donne had never even met her, as he states in several letters to friends, and he found himself embroiled in something of a dispute because of it, regretting that he had ever allowed them to be published. Not a lot less hyperbole, but more tact, was used in his poetry for Mrs Herbert and the Countess of Huntingdon, and it is a poem to the latter, 'Man to Gods image,

Eve, to mans was made', which provides us with some interesting material to consider. Keeping in mind its function as flattery, read it before continuing with the chapter.

We are not going to examine this poem in the same way as *Twicknam Garden*, examining specific usages of religious imagery; rather, what should concern us is the overall theme and how it is framed. The poem acknowledges very self-consciously its own status as flattery, and attempts to deny it with typical wit:

> If you can thinke these flatteries, they are,
> For then your judgement is below my praise,
> If they were so, oft, flatteries worke as farre,
> As Counsels, and as farre th'endeavour raise.
>
> (ll. 49–52)

None the less, the degree of praise involved is quite astonishing. The Countess is compared to a comet and a miracle; the Star of Bethlehem itself and even the sun. From her 'all vertues flow' (l. 45), and in praising her Donne is not only doing God's will, 'And all these gifts confess'd, which hee instill'd' (l. 63), but as her eulogist he is merely the 'Speaker of the universe' (l. 66). In its entirety the poem hymns the Countess as a woman wholly imbued with God's grace and goodness, the embodiment of pure virtue:

> She guilded us: But you are gold, and Shee;
> Us she inform'd, but transubstantiates you;
>
> (ll. 25–6)

The same crucially religious term we saw employed in *Twicknam Garden*, here invites us to compare the Countess with Christ himself. What are we to make of this outrageous hyperbole? How can we accommodate it with our developing understanding of his poetry, and the sincerity and depth of intellect so much of his verse exhibits?

One possible clue lies in the following verse where Donne provides us with various ways of looking at the Countess:

> So you, as woman, one doth comprehend,
> And in the vaile of kindred others see;

To some ye are reveal'd, as in a friend,
And as a vertuous Prince farre off, to mee.

(ll. 41–4)

Her husband sees her as a woman, while children and other relations regard her as kin. Still others are fortunate enough to see her as a friend, but it is the way Donne sees her which should most interest us. His secretive marriage to Anne More hurled him out of the powerful circles he had worked so hard to enter, until his ordination brought him some stability of income and success. For 14 years he sought financial help from friends and benefactors to support a constantly growing family in difficult conditions. It is not at all surprising then, even when he had become a successful and admired clergyman, that he saw his relationship with such people in these terms. The aristocrats he sought financial help from were indeed 'farre off' and liked to maintain that distance. The Countess of Bedford, however keen a supporter of Donne's, let it be publically known that she disapproved of his being ordained. If wealthy aristocrats had use of his poetic talent, and could furnish him with either money or advancement, Donne was not the least bit hesitant to provide them with what they wanted. In fact all his efforts to win support during those years did eventually bear fruit in the form of his ordination and appointment as Dean of St Paul's. It is important to keep in mind that his life was not that of a professional writer by any means, and he only really found a proper channel for his ambition in the Church. Poetry was always for Donne a rather embarrassing weakness. Is it then at all surprising that he could turn it to such obvious use when necessary? Should we be surprised if he uses the same techniques, images and ideas which proved so successful in the poetry we now study and admire? If he was fortunate enough on occasions to be able to turn his skill to his advantage and make some money, it is not the least surprising that he turned to familiar, tried and tested ground to do so. A second reading through the poem will reveal a whole host of familiar images and ideas.

The problem raises all sorts of interesting questions about patronage and the arts. How does a patron's distance or involvement affect the work itself? What happens when the state decides to become a patron? If Donne was a commercial poet, we can at least be grateful that he was one only on rare occasions.

The poem to The Countess of Huntingdon does at least end on a note we will be able to recognise in his more sincere, divine verse:

> I was your Prophet in your younger dayes,
> And now your Chaplaine, God in you to praise.
>
> (ll. 69–70)

In praising her, he was in fact only praising God.

We can now move onto the Divine Poems themselves, completing this chapter with a detailed analysis of three of the *Holy Sonnets*. Most of this group of sonnets were written in 1609–10, before he was ordained, which should remind us of the error in thinking of Donne's ordination as some kind of watershed between love poetry and divine poetry. They are some of the most written-about poems in the language, and students seeking further reading will find a fascinatingly diverse range of criticism on offer. But as is our normal practice, we will begin with the poems themselves and look at them closely, using the information and techniques we have developed so far to reach a level of confident understanding. Each sonnet appears before its analysis, and you should read them as carefully and responsively as possible before pursuing that analysis. They are intensely personal poems, as different from the vacuous flattery of, 'Man to Gods image, *Eve*, to mans was made,' as one could imagine.

Holy Sonnet I

> Thou hast made me, And shall thy worke decay?
> Repaire me now, for now mine end doth haste,
> I runne to death, and death meets me as fast,
> And all my pleasures are like yesterday;
> I dare not move my dimme eyes any way,   5
> Despaire behind, and death before doth cast
> Such terrour, and my feebled flesh doth waste
> By sinne in it, which it t'wards hell doth weigh;

Onely thou art above, and when towards thee
By thy leave I can looke, I rise againe;   10
But our old subtle foe so tempteth me,
That not one houre my selfe I can sustaine;
Thy Grace may wing me to prevent his art,
And thou like Adamant draw mine iron heart.

We are not confronted here, as so often in the *Songs and Sonnets*, with difficult vocabulary or complex images. Only his use of 'Adamant' in the last line, an archaic term for a magnet, might need elucidation. Neither is the syntax especially complex. The first line forms a clear, single sentence in the form of a question, and although the remainder of the poem is also a single, clearly constructed sentence, it does not proceed by ellipsis and is punctuated into units we can comprehend readily. Successful analysis here relies much more heavily on tone, rhythm and most importantly, on our intellectual grasp of the ideas themselves.

The sonnet opens, for example, with a dramatic question addressed directly to God in the second person. Many of the *Holy Sonnets* adopt the same, intensely personal tone of private reflection or prayer. A number of scholars have pointed out that in them, Donne was greatly influenced by, if not actively employing, the spiritual exercises devised by the Jesuit Ignatius Loyola, exercises which guided the individual by concentrating one's thought on one's way of life and sins, and ultimately the agony and suffering of Christ. A key element in them involved imagining some powerful scene and adding a prayer, often in the form of a conversation with God. Emotion was the fuel which drove the individual through the whole process, and Jesuits were fond of citing instances of hardened sinners brought to their knees in repentance through following the regimen. However consciously Donne employed Loyola's advice, and the critical debate sways erratically across a wide range of opinions, at present it is sufficient to know that he did, and that the *Holy Sonnets* often proceed via intensely emotional private debate and reflection.

The question Donne asks is also a magnificently central one, cutting through whole tomes of theological thinking in its directness. If God made him, why must he die? Why would God, the essence of love and all that is good, destroy that which he creates? It is the driving concern of most of the Divine Poems, Donne's search for eternal salvation. And immediately following it we hear the only answer Donne can ever find. 'Repair me now,' he pleads, save me through your grace. Whatever Donne's nominal religion at the time of composition, the notion of God's grace is an entirely Catholic one, and one we need to understand if we are to appreciate the fierce anxiety and desperation which ebbs and flows throughout the Divine Poems. For the Catholic, earthly life is a journey to heaven in which God can play a very active part. In the holy sacraments, from the moment of baptism, the Catholic soul receives God's gift of grace, and it is precisely this gift which saves the fallen soul from damnation. The sinful nature of man is never in doubt, but the Catholic abides in the comforting knowledge that God is infinitely kind, infinitely forgiving and seeks only our salvation. God rewards our good deeds and acts of Christianity with grace, the very means by which he conveys his love. Possessed of free will, we can therefore win our own salvation.

For the Protestant, no such route to bliss was possible. Critical of the Mass and other sacraments as near blasphemy, wholly incredulous of a spiritually competent clergy, the Protestant soul had only one means to salvation: his own faith. However, faith meant far more than believing in God. As Milton knew, even Satan possessed that type of faith. It was the belief in one's own salvation, the absolute acceptance of Christ as your saviour. But under the influence of Calvin it became something shockingly less simple and more threatening. Far from being able to win God's approval, the Protestant could do absolutely nothing on this earth to affect the fate of his soul. God had predetermined the fate of everyone's soul and no amount of good deeds or spiritual exercises could alter that. Grace did not exist. In the puritan mind, man was a woefully corrupt creature. Such severity caused enormous anguish and self-torment amongst intellectual Protestants, Donne included, since it presented them with an insoluble dilemma. If you can do nothing to win God's favour, and the fate of your soul is already determined, how can you escape damnation? Yet if you desire salvation, how can you not reflect on the state of your spiritual health? When Donne adopted the church of the state, immense anxiety and doubt were part of the price he paid. The *Holy Sonnets* reflect this very closely, and it is there even in the very first two lines of the first.

Envisaging his own death being close, he uses repetition ('now' and 'death') to stress the urgency and heighten the sense of desperation he feels when, 'all my pleasures are like yesterday' (l. 4). His image of running to meet death, and the realisation that death is racing to embrace him, strikes such fear into his soul that he is transfixed, and can look neither before nor behind. Weakened by age, his eyes are 'dimme' and his body aged, not by mere time, but by sin itself,

> and my feebled flesh doth waste
> By sinne in it, which it t'wards hell doth weigh;
>
> (ll. 7–8)

which drags him down towards hell. The sestet then begins with the faintest glimmer of hope:

> Onely thou art above, and when towards thee
> By thy leave I can looke, I rise againe;
>
> (ll. 9–10)

The Protestant is drawn down to hell by sin, while the Catholic still sees in God the loving figure who gives him 'leave' to look up and find relief from the overpowering despair. Yet subject to temptation by Satan, he can barely maintain this spirtual health an hour. Finally, in the closing couplet, it is again grace which provides his only hope. God's grace may lift him above the devil's 'art' and draw him heavenwards as a magnet draws iron. The image of his 'iron heart', underlining his sense of sinful unworthiness, is something we will see more of as we examine other Divine Poems.

The sonnet ends with Donne hopeful of God's grace. Nothing else presents itself as a means to salvation here, and the overpowering tone of despair and sense of his own weakness combine to create a poignant prayer. The poem is a far cry from the witty, elaborate invitations to pleasure, or complaints about the loss of it, which we have been analysing in the *Songs and Sonnets*.

Holy Sonnet XIII, 'What if the present were the worlds last night?', begins from a very similar position. But more reliant as we now are on using tone and rhythm to guide our analysis, it presents us with some curious problems.

Holy Sonnet XIII

What if this present were the worlds last night?
Marke in my heart, O Soule, where thou dost dwell,
The picture of Christ crucfied, and tell
Whether that countenance can thee affright,
Teares in his eyes quench the amazing light,   5
Blood fills his frownes, which from his pierc'd head fell.
And can that tongue adjudge thee unto hell,
Which pray'd forgivenesse for his foes fierce spight?
No, no; but as in my idolatrie
I said to all my profane mistresses,   10
Beauty, of pitty, foulnesse onely is
A signe of rigour: so I say to thee,
To wicked spirits are horrid shapes assign'd.
This beauteous forme asures a pitious minde.

As in the first sonnet, we are not barred from understanding by elaborate images or complex syntax. We have already learned that one of the informing practices behind the composition of the *Holy Sonnets* was the contemplation of the suffering Christ, and it is clearly central to this poem. Imagining that the world is to end this very night, Donne forces himself to think on Christ's agony and death on the cross, in order to understand the state of his own soul. It is worth recalling that, in Donne's age, the notion that the end of the world was indeed nigh was not at all uncommon. Here Donne states it with alarming simplicity in the opening line. He then begins a conversation with his own soul, again something we have learned formed a part of Loyola's spiritual exercises. He instructs his soul to study 'the picture of Christ crucified', hoping it will generate enough fear to make him penitent and worthy of salvation, 'Whether that countenance can thee affright' (l. 4). We should also note where Donne locates his soul. Interestingly it is in his heart, not his mind, both words commonly in use throughout his poetry. What does this imply? If we think back to the passionate drive of *Satyre* III, where Donne imagined religious faith as a matter of pure intellect and hard thinking:

> On a huge hill,
> Cragged, and steep, Truth stands, and hee that will
> Reach her, about must, and about must goe;
> And what the hills suddennes resists, winne so;
>
> (*Satyre* III, ll. 79–82)

we should be able to appreciate that a major change has taken place in his understanding of faith and its pursuance. Deeper into his religious life and journey, older and wiser, ironically, all that hard thinking has taken him to a point where the heart, not the mind, is the trusted organ. Donne's Catholicism again informs his poetry as he envisages his relationship with a loving God. It is Catholicism also which enables him to use, 'the picture of Christ crucified,' so readily, since images of the agony of the Christ play such a key part in the iconography of any Catholic church. Every Catholic church contains tableaux, the 14 stations of the cross, which adorn the walls, acting as a constant reminder of the events leading to the Resurrection. Single depictions of the dying Christ, in the form of paintings or sculptures, are of course the subject-matter for some of the greatest artists of the Renaissance and later.

So it is not an especially elaborate or metaphysical image for Donne to then see, 'Teares in his eyes quench the amazing light' (l. 5), as Christ looks to his Father in heaven in his agony. And the same is true of the subsequent image where he pictures the blood streaming from the wounds made by the crown of thorns filling 'his frownes' (l. 6). That Christ is frowning is crucial to Donne's thinking, since it is his own soul which is at stake here and Christ is judging him. What follows is a similar question to the one which opened the first sonnet, and again it is a Catholic mind which frames it. Is Christ really capable of sending Donne's soul to hell when even on the cross he forgave his murderers? The infinite mercy of God is something so deeply ingrained in Donne's pysche, he cannot quite shake it off. Even when an ordained and brilliant apologist for his adopted faith, the doubts persisted, as we will see in later poems. Here he struggles openly, since he is acutely aware of his own sinful nature, as the final sestet of the poem makes clear. It is in this sestet that we find the curious problems.

Faced with this vital question of whether Christ will damn him or not, the repetitious 'No, no' seems obviously unequivocal, yet, if he was so sure, would he need the comfort of repetition? That his doubts and fears remain is crucial to the whole poem, otherwise it would read as a wholly confident declaration of spiritual health. In seeking to find proof of God's unlimited capacity for mercy as evident in Christ's image, Donne employs an analogy which in itself is reminiscent of some of the more puzzling sections of the *Songs and Sonnets*, and which openly sends us back to them. We can analyse this difficult section using the now familiar technique of noting the structure through isolating the key words as has been done below:

> No, no; **but** as in my idolatrie
> I said to all my profane mistresses,
> Beauty, of pitty, foulnesse onely is
> A signe of rigour: **so** I say to thee,
> To wicked spirits are horrid shapes assign'd.

(ll. 9–13)

If the passage remains unclear, add speech marks around the imaginary direct speech. Turning back to the wayward days of his youth and his apparently busy pursuance of sex, which is implied by the plurality of mistresses involved, Donne calls it 'idolatrie'. The term directs us to the heart of the *Holy Sonnets* because the use of religious images for worship was one of the key accusations levelled by Protestants against Catholics. It is also fascinating since Donne seems to show no awareness at all of the possible contradiction in his using 'The picture of Christ crucified', in the opening part of the poem (in Protestant terms, idolatry), and his dismissal of his youthful sex life in exactly the same terms. The contrast he wants us to see is that between his former life, the one dedicated to pursuing women, which was idolatrous, and his religious life now. It should be evident from this where much of the habit of describing Donne's poetic life in two phases: secular and religious, came from. Yet we know from earlier in this chapter that he was writing *Satyre* III when he was still only 21 and presumably knee-deep in 'profane mistresses'.

What Donne actually said to them all is also problematic. The difficulty is created by the kind of ellipsis we have met before:

> Beauty, of pitty, foulnesse onely is
> A signe of rigour:
>
>   (ll. 11–12)

What he intends is for us to understand that as 'foulnesse' (by which he means something greater than mere ugliness) is a sign of feminine harshness, so beauty indicates pity. The implication is that, just as he always asserted beautiful women were capable of pity in love, and ugly ones were less forthcoming, so evil spirits are given vile shapes by God. It is important to note that is where the sentence, and the thought, ends. The last line of the poem refers us back to Christ's face on the Cross, and there Donne finds both the beauty, and most importantly the pity, he seeks so desperately.

What we make of this analogy, how shocked or persuaded we are by his linking Christ's dying face with the faces of his ex-beautiful mistresses, is now up to us. Undoubtedly the argument he refers to, his assuring beautiful women that their beauty signifies sexual compliance, is one we can hardly question after analysing so many of the *Songs and Sonnets*. As an invitation to that discussion, it is worth noting that the argument throughout relies on the use of visual representations, essentially the human face, and so there is something very consistent about the leap from Christ to Christine.

The final sonnet for analysis in this chapter is *Sonnet* XIV. Read it through carefully, bearing in mind Coleridge's opinion from our work on *Satyre* III, and make sure you pay special attention to the rhythm.

Sonnet XIV

Batter my heart, three person'd God; for, you
As yet but knocke, breathe, shine, and seeke to mend;
That I may rise, and stand, o'erthrow mee,'and bend
Your force, to breake, blowe, burn and make me new.
I, like an usurpt towne, to'another due,   5
Labour to'admit you, but Oh, to no end,
Reason your viceroy in mee, mee should defend,
But is captiv'd, and proves weake or untrue.
Yet dearely 'I love you,' and would be loved faine,
But am betroth'd unto your enemie: 10
Divorce mee,'untie, or breake that knot againe,
Take mee to you, imprison mee, for I
Except you'enthrall mee, never shall be free,
Nor ever chast, except you ravish mee.

We should have noticed the unusual rhythm of lines 2 and 4, where the lists hold the poem up. In each case the effect is subtly different. Having once more begun in a very dramatic fashion by using the violent image, 'Batter my heart', which is entirely in keeping with the 'iron heart' we noted in *Sonnet* I, Donne then finds words whose violence is limited and a rhythm to match the less severe idea of God's generous beneficence, almost gently remonstrating with his soul. The emphasis which falls on 'seeke' is especially marked, and echoes the sense of God as forgiving. In contrast, the rhythm of line 4, with its harsh sounds and almost horrific images, when one considers they are drawn from the proceedings of the torture chamber, stresses the cruelty and desire for punishment Donne feels. So overwhelming is his sense of unworthiness, only by such severe means can he envisage his salvation. Between these two lines comes the obvious paradox, 'That I may rise, and stand, o'erthrow mee', where only by being assaulted by God can he imagine himself worthy of God's attention.

Developing the idea of violent assault, he employs a conceit we might regard as more typical from our analysis of the *Songs and Sonnets*, since it is both elaborate and witty. Like a town taken over, 'usurpt', by a foreign power, yet anxious to assure its rightful possessors re-entry, he struggles to 'admit' God into his 'iron heart'. That he sees his predicament in military terms is strong evidence for the Protestant despair several critics have traced and outlined in his divine poetry. The emotional cost is carried by the exclamation, 'but Oh, to no end', where failure appears to accompany all his efforts to allow God in. The cause of this failure is a fascinating one since it sends us so confidently back to *Satyre* III and to *Sonnet* XIII. Donne's apotheosis of the intellect in *Satyre* III has become its opposite here, where 'Reason' is the barrier to unity with God. Yet Donne calls reason God's 'viceroy in mee', the very part of his humanity which should lead him towards God. It is a barrier because in this poem, his intellect betrays him. It is 'captiv'd, and proves weake or untrue', the clear implication being that Donne's resistance to temptation is low and that Satan all too easily distracts him. His immediate repetition of 'mee' (1.7) underlines the anxiety he feels. In fact he uses the word 'mee' nine times in this sonnet, which in itself highlights the overwhelming tone of frustrated communication with a voiceless God it attempts.

Again the sestet is separated by both rhythm and sense. Faced with the knowledge of his own weakness he quickly swings back towards God and our sense of his frustration and pain increases, 'Yet dearely' I love you,' and would be loved faine', where 'faine', as elsewhere, means readily or willingly. The military imagery now gives way momentarily to an image drawn directly from the previous line where Donne sees his relationship with God as one of love. Once more his sense of his own sinfulness leads him to describe himself as Satan's own, 'But am betroth'd unto your enemie' (l. 10), and only through more startling paradox can he see his way out. He urges God to act for him, where 'Divorce mee,'untie, or breake that knot againe,' applies to his betrothal to Satan. Our understanding of the final couplet might be limited by his usage of 'enthrall' which in Donne's age had an older meaning of 'to enslave', while its more modern sense of 'bewitch' is inappropriate. The most startling paradox, he returns to the imagery of lovers for, and saves for the final line, 'Nor ever chast, except you ravish mee.' Only through rape can he find innocence and purity. A sentiment which sits uncomfortably in the stomachs of contemporary feminist critics, one of whom, referring to her death in childbirth, described his wife Elizabeth (*sic*) More as 'a victim of his lust.'[3]

Finally, we might try an interesting experiment and read this sonnet, *minus* the first six words, to any willing listener and then ask them what they think they were listening to. If they say anything spiritual or religious at all, they haven't been listening. What makes this sonnet so significant and fascinating is it unequivocal use of the conventions and language of love poetry to deal with a spiritual dilemma. How conscious was Donne of this trait? Was he simply using the language and imagery which came most naturally to him, or was he deliberately playing with an awareness of this duality and trying to shock?

To summarise this chapter, we have seen in Donne's love poetry how instinctively he could resort to religious imagery. It appears the same can be said of his divine poetry. We have attacked the temptation to divide his work into two distinct areas, secular and religious, but at the same time seen symptoms of his changing religious view throughout his poetry. We have also noted his ability to function as a commercial writer and that the resulting poetry, especially in its use of hyperbole, raises questions of sincerity elsewhere in his verse.

There is an even more intriguing psychological line of argument we do not have space here to pursue, but perhaps in both his secular and divine verse he was in effect seeking the same quintessentially human prize, love.

Suggested Work

- Read all of the *Holy Sonnets* in sequence in order to gain a sense of their commonality and equip yourself for critical debate on their sequentiality and unity.

- Read *To Sir Henry Goodyer* and examine closely exactly how Donne exhorts his friend to improve. How does it differ in tone to *To the Countess of Huntingdon*? How does his advice accord with the image of himself we find in the *Holy Sonnets*?

- Read *A Hymne to Christ, at the author's last going into Germany,* and locate and evaluate the imagery which combines divine love with sexual love.

- Read *To the Countess of Bedford, Honour is so sublime* . . . and evaluate it as flattery or genuine spiritual advice.

7

Divine Poetry

In this final chapter of analysis we will examine some of the poems which have won Donne a reputation as a religious poet second only to Milton. The history of the term 'Metaphysical' when applied to Donne is dealt with in Part II of this book, but the term seems apt even without that critical history, since Donne is unique amongst English poets for the sincerity and depth with which he contemplates his relationship with his God and the universe. We might even be surprised when we reflect that, in the entire canon of English poetry, no other poet shows such concern for the state of his spiritual health. Whether we conclude this says more about Donne than it does about English poets is a matter for much broader critical debate.

By now we should be comfortable with our methods of analysis, and the reading of the first poem, *Good Friday, 1613. Riding Westward*, should strike us as a familiar experience. If after our reading we were to quickly note down characteristics we have met before, the list might include: elaborate conceits; provocative use of paradox; a rhythm determined by sense; a tightly disciplined control of structure; and a frequent use of questions and hyperbole. There are other features, of course, but this list illustrates how much we may have assimilated from previous chapters. We can use a combination of techniques from Chapters 1 and 2 to deal with the opening of this poem. It begins with a lengthy, complex sentence which we need to appreciate as a unit, and we can do this by isolating the words which control the structure in bold type. It also involves some contemporary astrology which needs some elucidation here, although the movement of the spheres has also been dealt with in Chapters 1 and 2. The whole opening sentence is reproduced below:

> **Let** mans Soule be a spheare, and then, in this,
> The intelligence that moves, devotion is,
> **And as** the other Spheares, by being growne
> Subject to forraigne motions, lose their owne,
> And being by others hurried every day,
> Scarce in a yeare their naturall forme obey:
> Pleasure or businesse, **so**, our Soules admit
> For their first mover, and are whirled by it.
>
> (ll. 1–8)

Donne establishes a conceit from the start by making his soul a sphere. As each sphere has a controlling angel, or intelligence which directs it, the controlling intelligence which moves man's soul should be devotion. However, just as the spheres are subject to the movements of other spheres and therefore change their course, so his soul is subject to other pressures, namely 'Pleasure or businesse,' and is diverted accordingly. My prosaic version, wooden in the extreme, highlights once more something essential to appreciate about poetry and the way it works. Donne's elegant, fluent sentence conveys the idea not only with more economy and skill, but with beauty and some degree of grace. As previously, we have shown the key structural words which dictate the two halves of the analogy in bold type. If we read the whole aloud, stressing them heavily, the sense should become even clearer.

The dramatic situation is a very singular one, as the title suggests. The poem is also one for which we fortunately have very good documentary evidence dealing with its composition. It was written in 1613, after Donne had been staying at the country estate of his friend, Sir Robert Goodyer in Polesworth, Staffordshire. From there he rode westwards to Montgomery Castle, some 65 miles, to stay with another friend. He wrote the poem during the journey and sent it to Goodyer, even before reaching Montgomery. The significance of the day is of course that it is the day of Christ's crucifixion. When a Catholic, Donne's entire year would have revolved around this day.

Easter is the central period of the liturgical calendar, and, for an Anglican in the seventeenth century, it would have had hardly less importance. If we are to understand the poem at all, we do need to register that difference from our contemporary world. For Donne, Good Friday was the one day in the year when death beckoned. At the time of writing Donne was 41 years old and close to ordination. 'Hence is't,' he says, that he is journeying west, 'when my Soules forme bends towards the East' (l.10).

What this means in spiritual terms he makes clear in the next sentence, through the witty oxymoron 'rising set', which relies on our perceiving the pun on 'Sunne', where Christ, the son of God, is the key element. Not only would Donne see a setting sun, he would see the image of Christ dying on the Cross. That image reminds him of why Christ died. His Resurrection brought the possibility of salvation, 'endlesse day', and without it 'Sinne had eternally benighted all' (l. 14). Satan's triumph in corrupting man in the Garden of Eden would have led to his eternal damnation. 'Christ died so that we might be saved' takes us, with Donne, to the very heart of Christian faith. If the events of Easter are not as told in the Gospels, then countless human souls have been wasting the last two millenia. A harsh but entirely justified way of stating it, the point being that, for Donne, there is absolutely no doubt at all about those truths. The doubt is about something else entirely.

Having stated the dramatic situation clearly, and declared himself guilty, he cleverly reverses our expectation and states, 'Yet dare I'almost be glad, I do not see' (l. 15) the image of Christ crucified. Why? we are forced to ask, even as he provides the answer:

> Who sees God's face, that is selfe life, must dye?
> What a death were it then to see God dye?
>
> (ll. 17–18)

There is a particular Biblical reference intended here, Exodus, xxxiii: 20, where we are reminded that it is death to see God's face, and Donne's conceit plays on the idea that to witness the Crucifixion was indeed to watch God die. Again employing direct Biblical references, where the earth is God's footstool in Isaiah, lxiv:1, and where

Matthew's Gospel account of the Crucifixion records that both an eclipse and an earthquake attended Christ's moment of death, Donne reminds us that so dreadful was that event, nature itself, God's 'Lieutenant', rebelled.

The next section of the poem builds on the juxtapostion he has created between the vastness of the event and his own sense of weakness and insignificance. The attributes he gives to God stress his immensity, and each is contrasted with an aspect of the crucifixion which makes the torture and death of Christ obscene. God's hands 'span the Poles', they tune 'all spheares at once', and yet are they to be seen nailed to the cross? God is both 'endlesse height' and 'our Antipodes', and is he then to be 'Humbled below us?' His blood, 'The seat of all our Soules,' spilt on the ground of Calvary makes 'durt of dust' (l. 27), an unusually sensual image for Donne but one which seems to arise from the necessity here of actually picturing the crucifixion. As does the following image of Christ's skin, the human form adopted by God 'for his apparell', being 'rag'd and torne?' by his tormentors. In his ceaseless search for excess, Donne then contrasts all these by the most human and intriguingly Catholic of images:

> If on these things I durst not looke, durst I
> Upon his miserable mother cast mine eye,
> Who was God's partner here, and furnish'd thus
> Halfe of that Sacrifice, which ransom'd us?
>
> (ll. 29–32)

The role and status of Mary, the mother of Christ, was something vehemently disputed between Catholics and Protestants, and only a Catholic mind could have envisaged her as Donne does here, one 'Halfe of that Sacrifice'. It is a powerful idea, bringing the tragedy which he has placed so carefully on its proper, immense plane, down to the human level of a grieving mother, forced to witness her only son's torture and ignominious death. In its essentially paradoxical nature, the death of man and God, the Crucifixion is a subject guaranteed to attract Donne.

The calm, alliterative rhythm of the subsequent line, 'Though

these things, as I ride, be from mine eye' (l. 33), takes us out of the
visualisation and into the concluding reflective section of the poem.
Though absent from his sight, the scenes are firmly entrenched in
his memory. His faith simply cannot allow him to ignore or forget
them, which is why he turns the idea so cleverly in line 35, where his
memory's directed gaze becomes Christ's. Donne's sense of guilt
drives him to describe Christ looking down at him from the Cross
while he turns his back to receive 'Corrections, till thy mercies bid
thee leave' (l. 38). As in the *Holy Sonnets* we have analysed, Donne
feels a need to be punished by God, a desire he frequently renders as
a submission to violence, abuse or even torture. If we recall the part
played in his youth by the Jesuits, and that he wrote an attack on the
whole business of martyrdom, *Pseudo-Martyr*, we may see where this
desire originates. Some critics have argued forcefully that Donne's
pleas for punishment in the Divine Poems directly reflect the gap he
felt existed between his own achievements, and the acts of the
martyrs. Because he was also so dramatically intent on saving his
soul, the instant canonisation afforded by the Catholic Church to
martyrs must have presented Donne with a galling intellectual
dilemma. However we choose to interpret his need for punishment,
it undoubtedly highlights his sense of his own fallibility and desire
for redemption.

In the final four lines this desire is voiced in clear and dramatic
terms, and once again it is only God's grace which can possibly save
him. Deformed by sin and rusty, only through God's active interven-
tion, 'O thinke mee worth thine anger' (l. 39), can he see his way
back to a state of spiritual health:

> Restore thine Image, so much, by thy grace,
> That thou may'st know mee, and I'll turne my face.

> (ll. 41–2)

Typically skilful in terms of structure, and in his handling of a
conceit, Donne brings the whole to an end by resolving the dramatic
dilemma he placed himself in at the poem's start, his riding west,
away from God. With God's grace he will be able to steer his soul
towards its proper destiny and look towards the east.

There is undoubtedly more we might say about this poem and two possible routes for further analysis indicate this. The poem's viewpoint, Donne's chosen way of looking at the Crucifixion and God's role, is interesting, and the poem's use of cosmological hyperbole equally so. You may wish to spend some time looking closely at these things before reading the second poem in this chapter, *A Hymne to God the Father*.

A Hymne to God the Father

I

Wilt thou forgive that sinne where I begunne,
   Which is my sin, though it were done before?
Wilt thou forgive those sinnes, through which I runne,
   And do run still: though I still do deplore?
     When thou hast done, thou hast not done,   5
     For I have more.

II

Wilt thou forgive that sinne by which I'have wonne
   Others to sinne? and, made my sinne their doore?
Wilt thou forgive that sinne which I did shunne
   A yeare, or two: but wallowed in, a score?   10
     When thou hast done, thou hast not done,
     For I have more.

III

I have a sinne of feare, that when I have spunne
   My last thred, I shall perish on the shore;
Sweare by thy selfe, that at my death thy sonne   15
   Shall shine as he shines now, and theretofore;
     And, having done that, Thou haste done,
     I feare no more.

Walton's *Life* tells us this poem was written when Donne was seriously ill, aged 51, having been Dean of St Paul's for two years. Donne arranged for the poem to be set to music and it was sung frequently by the choristers at St Paul's, as he was to survive this illness and live almost another eight years. An initial reading should have shown, primarily, that in structure, with its refrain in the last two lines of the first two verses, it is unusually lyrical for Donne, in spite of the few true songs in his *Songs and Sonnets*. Walton's account therefore, seems to be borne out by the rhythm of the poem itself. We may also have been struck by the contrast with *Good Friday, 1613. Riding Westward*.

Where the latter opened with an elaborate conceit sending us out into the larger universe, this poem has the immediate appeal and personal intensity of a prayer. Donne addresses his God in simple language, unadorned by anything except the repeated toying with his name. He begs forgiveness in a voice of calm resignation, brimming with humility and self-examination. Overall, what may most strike us is its simplicity, but how simple is it?

He begins by seeking forgiveness for his first sin, which though he can call his own, he still knows he was far from the first to commit. The interest comes from his punning on his name in line 2. It may be Donne's sin, but it was done before. The pun is quite a good one and might even raise a wry smile if it sneaks up on us, as some puns tend to do. How comfortably it lies in the body of a hymn or prayer is something we will reserve judgement on, since it is repeated throughout the poem. The pattern of the poem is established when he asks forgiveness for a second type of sin, those which, in spite of his repulsion, he commits habitually. If we recall how in *Holy Sonnet* I he imagined death rushing to meet him, we might see where his choice of verb comes from here, since 'runne' hints at how he is hastening his own end by sinning. But it also allows him the oxymoron, 'run still' (l.4), which works even more effectively in highlighting the aimlessness and failure of such habitual sins which keep him from progressing, holding him still on his spiritual journey.

The most open use of the pun on his name occurs at the end of the first verse, and is perhaps not as simple as at first thought. Firstly there is the paradox in God having, and not having, 'done' and Donne. God may think he has finished forgiving, but Donne has more to confess. This implied admission of guilt beyond God's knowledge is really astonishing since he is denying God's omniscience, yet simultaneously poignant because it allows him to prostrate himself in all his weakness before God. So instinctive is his use of hyperbole, even here during the intense self-examination involved in this prayer, Donne has to be even more sinful than God can know. It is also hard to resist the temptation to wonder about the use of 'more' to end all three verses. The abrupt short line makes it emphatic, it is the only word carrying any weight at all in those three concluding lines, and while he is playing so intently with his own name, it seems strange to think he would not be aware of the pun on his dead wife's. Anne had died only six years before and, having taken her from a life of plenty and comfort into one of poverty and distress (surely the likely situation of bearing and mothering so many children), which only ended in her death through giving birth yet again, he must have felt quite extraordinary guilt. However tempting it is to speculate in this direction, it can only be speculation, since Anne More remains one of the most maddeningly enigmatic muses in English literary history.

Verse two restores the confessional list with sins which Donne knows have brought others to sin. His use of 'doore' (l. 8) is unclear in that he does not specify whether he sees it as a door to further sin, or to hell itself. That the poem belongs to his later years is again clear from the next type of sin which are sins he manages to avoid 'A yeare, or two' but wallows in for twenty. Some critics see this as further evidence for Walton's construction of his life as Jack Donne, the erotic adventurer, and Dr John Donne, the revered sermoniser and Dean. Catholics used to the conventions of the confessional would perhaps see something less drastic and far more familiar. The time spent before entering the confessional, reflecting on one's sins, gives rise to a tendency to recognise them and of course, name and categorise them. This is once again one of those aspects of culture and history we need to fully appreciate for us to analyse the poem at all successfully. Contemporary western culture has almost abolished sin. It is now something most of us are hardly aware of and may even be ignorant of. In a world where Satan was not only active but visibly so, where there were only two ultimate choices – heaven or hell – it was not so much a matter of life or death, it was a matter of eternal life or eternal damnation.

Donne's third verse begins with a poignantly personal sin, but one which we may not even understand. That sin is the sin of doubt: one which his Protestant contemporaries would have instantly recognised, and sympathised with. Donne fears that at the last, he will 'perish on the shore' (l. 14), precisely because of his lack of faith and trust in God. In a step of astounding boldness, he actually demands God 'Sweare by thy selfe,' that when he dies, Christ 'thy sonne' will 'shine as he shines now', and for ever. It is the same pun we saw in *Good Friday, 1613. Riding Westward*, but it exposes a crucial difference between the two poems. Whereas in the former, Donne's back was turned towards God and he needed Christ's admonition to be restored, here he is writing in a state of grace, under Christ's shining gaze, 'as he shines now'. The whole thought of *Good Friday, 1613. Riding Westward* was driven by Donne's unfitness to see, in his mind's eye, the Crucifixion, while here he is bathed in God's light and can end the poem confidently asserting the very trust in God which he admitted he lacked at the start of the verse. Once again what we encounter is the complex product of Donne's apostasy. The Protestant intellect wallows in doubt and anxiety which only the Catholic notion of God's grace appears able to resolve:

> And, having done that, Thou hast done,
> I fear no more.

> (ll. 17–18)

If prayers are personal attempts to communicate with God, then *A Hymne to God the Father* is surely a rather graceful and appealing prayer. Its superficial simplicity masks an elegant and skilful voicing of our common weaknesses and doubts, via a witty playing on his own name, which is remarkably well judged. Although we might see in the poem something typical in its obsession with Donne's ego, it would be churlish to describe that as arrogant amidst so much vulnerable honesty.

The final section of analysis follows, in which we will look at four of the *Holy Sonnets*. The detailed analyses of each employ methods and knowledge gained from all the previous chapters, and consolidate what we have learned about how to analyse Donne's difficult and demanding poetry. The first is *Sonnet* XVII, 'Since she whom I lov'd.'

Sonnet XVII

Since she whom I lov'd hath payd her last debt
To Nature, and to hers, and my good is dead,
And her Soule early into heaven ravished,
Wholly on heavenly things my mind is sett.
Here the admyring her my mind did whett   5
To seeke thee God; so streames do shew the head;
But though I have found thee, and thou my thirst has fed,
A holy thirsty dropsy melts mee yett.
But why should I begge more Love, when as thou,
Dost wooe my soule for hers; offering all thine: 10
And dost not only feare least I allow
My Love to Saints and Angels things divine,
But in thy tender jealosy dost doubt
Least the World, Fleshe, yea Devill putt thee out.

If we didn't have Walton's book to tell us, it would be fairly clear that Donne is writing here about his wife after her death. She died on 15 August 1617, seven days after she had given still birth to her twelfth or thirteenth child, biographers differ on which. She was only 33. Donne's epitaph for her describes her as, 'a woman most choice, most beloved and most loving, a wife most dear and chaste, a mother most pious, dutiful, self-sacrificing, and indulgent' and he was by her death, *dolore infans*, 'by grief made speechless.'[1] Not so speechless that he could not pen this elaborate and difficult poem as a result of her death. His use of 'ravished' (l. 3) to describe the way she has been taken up into heaven, as though God was a rival lover and has stolen her from him, might shock the newcomer to Donne, but should not at all surprise us. We may be confused by the imprecision of 'and to hers,' in line 2, but can resolve this by carefully locating the verb which accompanies it. The confusion is the result of ellipsis, as Donne has missed out the 'good' which is implied goes with 'hers'. Her death, in other words, is for both their goods, his and hers. Understanding this idea might be equally problematic to a newcomer, but in conjunction with the sexual imagery, the idea that her death is 'early' and that it has had the result of focusing his mind, 'Wholly on heavenly things' (l. 4), we should readily appreciate that her winning eternal life far outweighs any other good, and if it brings Donne closer to that elusive goal too, it is entirely for his too. Modern sensibilities might stiffen a little at this apparent lack of grief, but our knowledge of Donne and his age must override this and give us the informed response which more closely approximates to Donne's own readers. If we also consider the poem as one of the *Holy Sonnets,* a group which together are preoccupied with Donne's relationship with God and his desperate desire for salvation, then his positive response here to Anne's death becomes even less objectionable. We have already seen, in the Divine Poems, how he regards his spiritual life as one predominantly shadowed by weakness and doubt, only rarely infused with divine grace and confidence. This sonnet may seem unusual therefore in that Donne's fixity of purpose is so strong, his mind 'sett' unshakeably on heaven.

The praise of Anne implied already in her being 'ravished,' into heaven, continues in lines 5 and 6, where we are told that it was through 'admyring' her that Donne found his intellectual desire for God sharpened. 'Whett' is especially clever because although we tend today to use it only rarely, and then restricted to the sharpening of a tool or blade, it also has the secondary meaning to sharpen an appetite by a small taste. That secondary meaning is the primary one for Donne, as the subsequent image makes clear, 'so streames do shew the head' (l. 6). We may here recall the use Donne made of the image of a stream in *Satyre* III, 'As streames are, Power is' (l. 103), and find the difference instructive, since here the movement is in entirely the opposite direction and it is the stream which shows the way to the 'head', Anne who directed Donne to God. In *Satyre* III the stream weakens our hold, and sends us headlong into the sea to vanish and drown. It is a neat illustration of how agile Donne's poetic intellect was, where dramatically different usages of the same image occur. As we will discover in the second part of this study, some critics have sought to narrow Donne's use of imagery down and categorise it, rather than note the agility of his lithe mind.

As so often when most stimulated, Donne develops and expands the stream image in an unexpected way. But before we examine that, we will pursue a different aspect of his use of Anne to debate his relationship with God here. We have stressed that, for Donne, sexual imagery and religious imagery, far from being somehow incompatible morally, are almost interdependent. In a youthful poem about sexual desire he has no qualms at all about using religious ideas, and in the most earnest private communication between him and his God, sexual images abound. So what are we to make of the notion that his admiration for Anne fed his appetite for God?

On one level we can see he may be praising Anne's piety and goodness, something we noted from her epitaph, yet 'admyring', coming hot on the heels of 'ravished', cannot but make us think of his sexual desire for her too, and it is this which provides the key. In the sestet of the poem this becomes clearer as Donne continues by describing his relationship with God in terms of love. It is love he seeks and love which unites his relationship with God and with Anne. Love in this sonnet replaces the use of grace elsewhere, but they are essentially the same in Donne's mind, both signifying God's readiness to grant him forgiveness and assure his soul of salvation. The link between Anne and God which drives this sonnet might also make perfect sense viewed against the guilt we noted in *A Hymne to God the Father*, where we speculated on what part his love and life with Anne had played in that. Describing Anne, (who must surely in his life have sated his greediest sexual desires and energies), as the stream who showed him God, is possibly one way for him to soothe a painfully guilty conscience, made even more painful by her recent death.

Although he states Anne has led him directly to God, and God has responded, 'thou my thirst has fed', the poem continues with Donne greedy for more via an image we have seen before in our analysis of *A Nocturnal upon St Lucies Day* in Chapter 5. 'A holy thirsty dropsy melts mee yett', he states, forcefully ending the octet but leaving us waiting for an explanation. It comes immediately and, as we have intimated earlier, it is for God's love he thirsts. Yet the remainder of the sonnet, the entire sestet in effect, resists easy explanations and forces us to think for ourselves. It is the kind of passage which tests our knowledge and analytical abilities most severely, and we will approach it here as we have done in previous chapters, methodically yet thoughtfully. If we try to clarify the structure of this lengthy sentence by finding the key linking words, it helps us only so far in this case. The difficulty here is created largely by Donne's use of 'as' (l. 9). Because it is normally the first half of an analogy, we expect a 'so' to follow but don't get one, and nor do we get a synonym. Reading the passage stressing the bold words below, should make the structure clearer:

> **But** why should I begg more Love, **when as thou,**
> **Dost** wooe my soule for hers; offering all thine:
> **And dost** not only feare least I allow
> My Love to Saints and Angels things divine,
> **But** in thy tender jealosy **dost doubt**
> Least the World, Fleshe, yea Devill putt thee out.
>
> (ll. 9–14)

The initial statement is fair enough. Why does he beg more love, Donne asks, when he knows that God now courts Donne's soul for Anne's, and in return offers all his love. 'But why should I begg more Love' (l. 9), is balanced by 'offring all thine' (l. 10). The question is entirely rhetorical and is uttered more in a tone of calm acceptance than urgent demand, which is most easily understood by our placing heavy emphasis on 'when' (l. 9) as we read. Donne is nullifying the question by giving the reasons why it is unnecessary. Maintaining the state of grace he envisaged in line 4, he sees God as a tenderly jealous lover, whose jealousy has been aroused by two aspects of his life. As a Protestant he cannot now 'allow' his love to 'Saints and Angels' (l. 13), which was something he formerly could, as a Catholic. We already know one of the key criticisms Protestantism levelled at Catholicism was that its treatment of saints and martyrs amounted to idolatry. The second was in the rivalry posed by Anne where God takes her soul, fearing she might displace him in Donne's heart, 'Least the World, Fleshe, yea Devill putt thee out'(l. 14). If we hear in the poem's sestet, a tone of tender admonishment, where Donne gently corrects God for doubting him, we can see that the whole makes absolute sense as a response to the loss of Anne, whereas some critics have seen it as cruelly selfish and lacking all signs of grief. Donne has found a reason for Anne's death, and that reason is God's love. In such a state of mind, grief becomes simply irrelevant.

In contrast to this mild and poignant eulogy, now read *Sonnet* XI 'Spit in my face you Jewes,' and the analysis which follows.

Sonnet XI

Spit in my face you Jewes, and pierce my side,
Buffet, and scoffe, scourge, and crucifie mee,
For I have sinn'd, and sinn'd, and onely hee,
Who could do no iniquitie, hath dyed:
But by my death can not be satisfied   5
My sinnes, which passe the Jewes impiety:
They kill'd once an inglorious man, but I
Crucifie him daily, being now glorified.
Oh let mee then, his strange love still admire:
Kings pardon, but he bore our punishment.   10
And Jacob came cloth'd in vile harsh attire
But to supplant, and with gainfull intent:
God cloth'd himselfe in vile mans flesh, that so
Hee might be weake enough to suffer woe.

The opening is dramatically violent, and shocking, Donne substituting himself for Christ, and some critics have marked the arrogance of this. But we know that informing this group of sonnets are the spiritual exercises designed by Ignatius Loyola, and that a critical part of those involved using one's imagination to empathise deeply with the crucified Christ. Donne takes that instruction to its logical conclusion here, imaginatively seeking the same cruelty which his saviour suffered. Once again we may find modern sensibilities cloud our understanding, and using terms like masochism will not help us greatly because that is not the force which is driving the image. It is rather a profound desire to get closer to God which stimulates someone to attempt the spiritual exercises at all.

The opening is also interesting in its use of rhythm which succeeds in placing all the emphasis on Donne via the repetition of 'my' in line 1, and the stress on 'mee,' in line 2. Similarly he uses rhythm and repetition to emphasise how sinful he is in line 3, something we have observed already in *A Hymne to God the Father*. Consciousness of his own unworthiness nags at him throughout the Divine Poems, and in this sonnet it finds its home in exposing the ridiculousness of the initial wish. Donne may have 'sinned, and sinned' (l. 3), but it is Christ, the one sinless man in creation, 'Who could do no iniquity' (l. 4), who died. The following two lines may be difficult because of the use of 'satisfied' in line 5. Donne is using it in the sense of atonement, meaning that his death is not sufficient to make up for all the sins he has committed, and to reinforce this he assures us they 'passe the Jewes impiety', because Donne repeats them, knowingly. The element of imagination involved in Loyola's exercise can be seen again in the clever differentiation Donne makes between his own sin and the Jews. From their point of view, they merely 'killed once an inglorious man' (l. 7), a succinct image which contrasts pointedly with Donne's sinning nature, which means he crucifies him 'daily, being now glorified' (l. 8). It is a forceful way to end the octet, Donne reminding himself (and us) that in our privileged position since the Crucifixion and Resurrection, our sins are even more cruel and iniquitous.

That Donne is involved in some kind of spiritual exercise is virtually acknowledged by the tone which opens the sestet, 'Oh let me then' (l. 9), and the idea of his being made to reflect on where his thinking has brought him, 'His strange love still admire.' It is the immensity of God's love, the unqualified nature of his capacity to forgive us, which Donne is in awe of. Though kings may grant forgiveness in the form of pardons, God actually endured our punishment for us, and in a Biblical allusion to the story in Genesis xxvii, where Jacob disguises himself as his elder brother to seek favour with his father, Donne stresses the grotesque debasement involved in God's adopting human form as Christ, 'in vile harsh attire'. The final couplet elaborates this, emphasising the sacrifice involved in God's action, and in doing so bringing us back to the opening image of the Crucifixion. God adopted man's shape as Christ, in order that he could become, 'weak enough to suffer woe' (l. 14). It is difficult to see here how interpretations of this sonnet as arrogant or indicative of Donne's immense ego sound persuasive when all the final weight of the verse falls on the comparison between Christ and Donne: God and man. So astounding is the nature of God's sacrifice, the feeling most appropriate at the end of the poem is shame.

Perhaps Ignatious Loyola would have been more impressed than we are, but we should, none the less, appreciate the sentiment.

The next sonnet for analysis is *Sonnet* VI, 'This is my playes last scene.'

Sonnet VI

> This is my playes last scene, here heavens appoint
> My pilgrimages last mile; and my race
> Idly, yet quickly runne, hath this last pace,
> My spans last inch, my minutes latest point,
> And gluttonous death, will instantly unjoynt   5
> My body, and soule, and I shall sleepe a space,
> But my'ever-waking part shall see that face,
> Whose feare already shakes my every joynt:
> Then, as my soule, to'heaven her first seate, takes flight,
> And earth-borne body, in the earth shall dwell,   10
> So, fall my sinnes, that all may have their right,
> To where they'are bred, and would press me, to hell.
> Impute me righteous, thus purg'd of evill,
> For thus I leave the world, the flesh, and devill.

As with the majority of Donne's poems, we have no clear date for the composition of this sonnet, but whether it was written close to his death, or during a period of illness, as Walton tells us was true of the *Hymne to God my God, in my Sickness*, the dramatic power of the opening is very striking. Donne is facing death. There is nothing especially original about his use of the stage as an image for one's life, Shakespeare's Macbeth and Jacques make stunning use of the same convention, and what Donne does is use it merely as the first of a list. The list is one of finalities, each reinforcing the imminence of death. The items in the list are so straightforward they should not need enumerating at this stage, but we do need to note that he uses the word 'last' four times in the first four lines, which has the effect of leaving him little room for manoeuvre. So close to death does his imagination take him, there seems no time even for the kind of communication with God we have seen in other Divine Poems. We should also note the paradox in 'Idly, yet quickly runne' (l. 3), and the powerful way he personifies Death, 'gluttonous' and ready to 'instantly unjoynt' his body from his soul. The notion that the body and soul were separated at death until the Day of Judgement is one which exercised many theological minds, including St Augustine's, and Donne is not suggesting anything new in this. In the interim, Donne then imagines his soul, that 'ever-waking part' of him, meeting his Maker, and the syntax here may be a little awkward where 'Whose fear' (l. 8) clearly belongs to 'that face' (l. 7). It is not God who is afraid, of course, but Donne, and the sense is rather fear of whom. Yet again we see a division between the octect and sestet, not so much in terms of rhythm but in sense and content. Having created a state of tense anxiety where fear of God 'shakes' his 'every joynt' (l. 8), he now attempts to resolve it in the final lines of the poem.

Our analysis of the next four lines should benefit from a very clear comparison with work on *Sonnet* XVII, where Donne's use of 'as' without a subsequent 'so' or 'then' created some difficulty. Here the 'as' is followed by the expected 'so' as highlighted below, and the sense is therefore far less difficult:

> Then, **as** my soule, to'heaven her first seate, takes flight,
> And earth-borne body, in the earth shall dwell,
> **So**, fall my sinnes, that all may have their right,
> To where they'are bred, and would presse me, to hell.
>
> (ll. 9–12)

What Donne hopes, perhaps even prays, for here is that, as his soul and body separate, the former seeking its rightful home in heaven, his sins fall from his soul and, by so doing, fail to drag him down towards hell. He seeks reassurance in balance by deliberately paralleling 'her first seate,' with 'where they'are bred', and openly acknowledging the hope in this arrangement 'that all may have their right' (l. 11). His sins, having been bred in hell, should return there and leave his soul free.

The final couplet encapsulates something we have seen permeates the *Holy Sonnets*, Donne's desperate anxiety about his own salvation, something he inherited when he abandoned the Catholic Church of his birth for the Anglican Church of his state. Becoming not just a Protestant, but an acknowledged voice for Protestantism, which he deliberately did through early prose writings as much as in his later sermons, meant that he could not avoid some of the less comfortable consequences. Intrinsic doubt and anxiety about his own spiritual health was one of these, and in *Sonnet* VI we see that beautifully illustrated. In contrast to the frustrated intensity we see in other Divine Poems, here Donne's tone is resigned and poignantly honest. 'Impute me righteous', he asks God, where 'Impute' carries a very specific theological meaning of ascribing one quality to one person, by virtue of a similar quality in another. The appeal is once more directly to his God. As you are all goodness, he seeks to say, see that goodness in me and save my soul. Whereas in *Sonnet* XVII Donne envisaged God as jealous of the power, 'the world, the flesh, and devill', had over him, here they are unambiguously rejected.

There is one final intriguing aspect to this sonnet which may have come to our attention during the reading or analysis. Donne's use of 'unjoynt' and 'shakes my every joynt', and 'would presse me', would have raised, in the mind of his readers, associations to do with persecution and martyrdom, torture and execution, which probably evade modern readers. Disassembling skeletons while their owners were still using them was a favourite method of men employed by the state to handle the practicalities of persecuting Catholics, as was pressing them to death with weights, the fate of the first English martyr, Margaret Clitherow. Donne was born into times of intense civil and intellectual conflict made manifest in the cruellest, often most public manner. He had seen Catholics praying openly at the scene of execution in the hope that the newly made martyr would intercede for them with God, risking their own death by doing so, and the fate of his brother Henry (mercifully of the plague before the butchers could do their work) must have left an indelible stain on him. In his letters and sermons he repeatedly attacks martyrs as misled and deluded, and yet in all of this there is always something darkly guilty. There is no zealot like a convert, and in attacking the Jesuits and their attitude towards martyrs Donne was indeed zealous; yet very possibly what

Donne saw was men succeeding where he had failed. What if they really were granted instant saintliness? What if their faith, carried to the limit, actually bought them instant salvation? It would help explain the violence and cruelty of much of the imagery and his repeated demand for punishment in the Divine Poems.

As a final poem for analysis I have chosen one of Donne's most famous *Holy Sonnets* and one which, while drawing together some familiar threads, seems to give rise to some extremely homespun critical material. Read *Sonnet* X, 'Death be not proud,' before the final analysis of Part I.

Sonnet X

Death be not proud, though some have called thee
Mighty and dreadfull, for, thou art not soe,
For, those, whom thou think'st, thou dost overthrow,
Die not, poore death, nor yet canst thou kill mee.
From rest and sleepe, which but thy pictures bee,   5
Much pleasure, then from thee, much more must flow,
And soonest our best men with thee doe goe,
Rest of their bones, and soules deliverie.
Thou art slave to Fate, Chance, kings, and desperate men,
And dost with poyson, warre, and sicknesse dwell,   10
And poppie, or charmes can make us sleepe as well,
And better than thy stroake; why swell'st thou then?
One short sleepe past, wee wake enternally,
And death shall be no more; death, thou shalt die.

It takes a bold man to taunt death, but Donne opens the sonnet not just with a direct admonition, but with the astounding claim that he is immortal, 'nor yet canst thou kill mee' (l. 4). His method here, as elsewhere, is to establish an argument or conceit which challenges our thinking, and then explain or elucidate it. What Donne seeks to undermine in this opening is not, as we might initially think, that death is 'proud,' but that he is 'Mighty and dreadfull'. This is hardly the typical attitude or stance taken in the *Holy*

Sonnets. Death is neither frightening nor powerful: in fact, since those 'thou think'st, thou dost overthrow' (l. 3), do not die, he is also misguided. Donne then attempts to provide us with the reasoning which has allowed him to make this rash claim. Lines 5 and 6 are demanding until we see that he is making the verb 'flow' work for both death and 'rest and sleepe', so that knowing we gain pleasure from sleep and rest, which are merely 'pictures' of death, means death itself will offer even greater 'pleasure'. Next he exploits the platitude that the best die young, and therefore find both 'rest' and their 'soules deliverie' (l. 8). How this idea is adduced to his argument is unclear unless we recognise that he is implying, by using 'goe', that the best men choose this fate for themselves, their departure on this journey is an entirely willing one, and we should learn from their example. The use of 'deliverie' also makes us think of the birth of the soul that occurs at death when it is separated from the body, which not only emphasises the wisdom of those 'best men', but may even take us back to thoughts of martyrdom. How many young men had Donne seen or known of, who chose death and walked calmly to greet him on the scaffold?

The boldness of the argument continues in the sestet where Donne degrades death as far as possible, by making him a slave to 'Fate, Chance, kings, and desperate men' (l. 9), all having in common the crude ability to kill. Death is envisaged living with 'poyson, warre, and sicknesse', as though this too were somehow degrading, and drugs 'poppie, or charmes', trivial, flimsy objects, are equally effective in making us sleep as death. It is difficult at this point to fail to notice the contradiction Donne has woven for himself, where sleep now seems better than death, 'better than thy stroake' (l. 12), when in lines 5 and 6 he argued the opposite. And when he insists in deflating death again, 'why swell'st thou then?' (l. 12), it is death's pride which seems at issue, not his might or dread, which was not the case in the opening.

In the final couplet, with its controlled rhythm and confident alliteration in the last line, Donne dismisses the terrifying ogre of the Divine Poems and finds ease for his anxious soul. Between dying and eternal life is merely a 'short sleepe', and triumphantly he declares the end of Death, 'death, thou shalt die'.

However confused we view the argument of this sonnet, however muddled and unconvincing the thinking, and compared to most of Donne's verse the analogies here are, as he might have put it, 'to ayery thinnesse beate', we must surely be impressed by the confidence and power of the closing lines. We may even find the whole poem impressive merely through its ambition, but it is foolhardy in the extreme to see it as a watertight argument based on rational thinking. It is entirely in harmony with the other *Holy Sonnets* beneath its brash surface, because it voices so articulately its maker's anxiety, his desperate need to know.

So we can conclude that if in carrying out these analyses, we have found ourselves repeatedly puzzled or confused, forced to think, it is because what vitalised Donne was not the physical nature of the world around him, or the mechanics of other minds, but his own fierce desire to understand. What happens frequently in his verse is that we witness this attempt at understanding, however incomplete that effort is. Whether it is his hunger for sexual gratification, greed for love, or terrifying awareness of his own guilt, Donne never turns away from the difficulties they conceive, and, if we choose to read him, we are forced to think with him.

PART 2

THE CONTEXT

AND

THE CRITICS

8

John Donne's Life and Works

Both Donne's parents were Catholics. His father was a warden of the Ironmongers Company in the City, and was one of those influential Catholics who managed somehow to avoid government attention. His mother was the youngest daughter of the poet and playwright John Heywood, and Heywood's wife was the niece of Sir Thomas More. As a young, ambitious, well-connected young man, living with others of his kind in Lincoln's Inn, fresh from university where his faith had meant he was forbidden to graduate, John Donne none the less had access to the very heart of Elizabethan culture and power. He travelled, although precisely when and where are subject to dispute, although we do know that he fought with the Earl of Essex and Sir Walter Raleigh against the Spanish at Cadiz, famously witnessing the destruction of the Spanish flagship, the *San Felipe*, and her crew in the burning seas. By the age of 25 he had all the gifts and experience necessary for a stunning diplomatic career, and this appears to have been what he wished for himself when he was appointed chief secretary to Lord Keeper of the Great Seal, Sir Thomas Egerton. It was a privileged position, one which gave him knowledge of the central political events of the time. Donne was established at Sir Thomas's London home, York House, close to the Palace at Whitehall where he worked, and which was at the time the most influential social site in Europe. But the glittering career failed to materialise because, while living at York House, Donne fell in love with one of its occupants, Sir Thomas's niece, Anne More, the daughter of Sir George More whose seat was Loseley Park near Guildford.

Together with his apostasy, this relationship was one of the two most significant events in Donne's life as a man and a poet. However their relationship developed, the end result was that by 1602 Anne was almost certainly pregnant and they were secretly married. It was a disastrous act for Donne in terms of his career and future, but how it affected his poetic life, and consequently the body of love poetry he bequeathed us, can only be conjecture again. When Anne's father discovered that the 17-year-old daughter he had been grooming for a great match had secretly married a servant, and a Catholic one at that, he was incensed, and Donne's manner of explaining himself did not help. Donne wrote to him via the Earl of Northumberland, admitting to the marriage but arguing that the only reason they had not sought Sir George's consent was because they knew it would not be given. Donne wrote:

> I know no passion can alter your reason and wisdom, to which I adventure to commend these particulars: that it is irremediably done; that if you incense my Lord [Sir Thomas] you destroy her and me; that it is easy to give us happiness, and that my endeavours and my industry, if it please you to prosper them, may soon make me somewhat worthier of her.

The confidence Donne clearly had in his own ability and future is glaringly evident here, where, even in such danger, he strikes through the surface to the heart of the issue and seeks advancement. He did not get it. Sir George forced his reluctant brother-in-law, Donne's employer, to dismiss him and, within days, Donne was imprisoned in the Fleet prison. Anne was taken home, where presumably she had to deal with a furious father alone, but Donne's incarceration was brief due to the good offices of Sir Thomas. Although free, all his efforts to regain his position were in vain. At the age of 30, with a pregnant young wife, Donne faced years of penury and isolation by seeking help from the aristocratic friends he still had.

Friends did come to his aid, and he survived largely through their patronage and help until he had worked himself back into some favour with the then King James I, who, never quite satisfied with his youthful escapade, convinced Donne that his only hope of advancement was to enter the Church, which he finally did in 1621. There Donne found more food for his hungry intellect and, whatever the frame of mind he was in at the time of his ordination, he proved a kind and effective priest and famous preacher. His sermons figure amongst some of the most powerful and memorable in the language and there are few reasonably educated people who have not heard his famous injunction, 'And therefore never send to know for whom the bell tolls; it tolls for thee', or assertion, 'No man is an Island,' which come from the same sermon.

Anne died in 1617, in childbirth, and, although we know Donne was devastated, we know very little else about the woman who must have influenced his poetry. Where does the poetry itself belong in all of this? One of the ways educated nobleman of the time amused themselves was the composition of verse, and when circulated amongst friends, poetry became a way to influence people and win their respect. Donne undoubtedly earned a reputation in this way during his years after leaving university. And love poetry was considered almost a necessary part of courtship. In 1614 he had to write to a number of friends to obtain copies of his poems, because he had none of his own, and complained that it was more trouble to do that than to write them in the first place. Yet however strongly he dismisses his earlier, secular poetry, as in later life and sermons he did, it was the armoury he employed in his intellectual battle with the age, and we should be eternally grateful that it was so. His poetry has had far-reaching effects on numerous writers and the whole evolution of English poetry. Reading Donne's poetry takes one into the Jacobean social and spiritual arena with him. Though he rarely cares to open our eyes to the physical presence of the world around him, he nonetheless allows us intellectual access to it via the raw honesty of one of its most insightful participants. There is no escaping that Donne is a difficult poet. His writing has challenged critics and readers for over three centuries and stirred the imaginations of some our greatest poets, men like Coleridge and T.S. Eliot.

For a man who called his poetry 'ragges of verses' and 'evaporations of wit', and whose letters to friends repeatedly show him apologising or underplaying his skill, Donne was prolific. Whereas

Shakespeare as a historical figure is as tantalisingly evanescent as any great artist could ever be, Donne is much more solid, and the information we have about his life enhances, in fact teases, our response to his verse. However, his first biographer, Izaak Walton, knew Donne only in his final years and so, from the onset, that information has been slightly suspect, and in applying our knowledge of the man to the poetry, we still have to be extremely cautious. The single most significant person in his life, in view of how she affected its outcome, his wife Anne, wholly resists historical investigation in spite of intense critical interest and energy. But Donne was also a prolific letter-writer and cultivated a circle of close friends from his young manhood onwards, which enables us occasionally to hear his voice in a more domestic mode. His Jesuit education by some of the sharpest intellects of the age, and his ambition, combined to make him write some acerbic, absolutely contemporary prose works, and as an ordained Anglican minister and ultimately Dean of St Paul's, he earned a reputation as a brilliant sermoniser.

Although his biographers all correctly stress the devastation caused to his career by his elopement, and that his entry into the Church was reluctant to say the least, they mostly fail to see the point that a glance over his life reveals: that it was almost entirely spent writing. Whether intense religious diatribe or heartfelt personal letter, the activity was essentially the same, always beginning with an empty page and Donne's mind.

There are difficulties dating Donne's poems, but work done by editors like H.J.C. Grierson, the first to produce a thoroughly researched and still more or less definitive collection of his poetry, has helped to narrow things substantially. A few of the poems, and many of the verse letters bear dates, yet critics seem to find themselves repeatedly drawn to a comment attributed to Ben Jonson by his friend William Drummond of Hawthornden, who recorded their conversations in a short book. Jonson was supposed to have, 'Affirmeth Done to have written all his best pieces ere he was 25 years old.'[1] But 'best pieces' is as subjective a view as one could find, and since from the same source we learn that Jonson knew part of *The Calme* off by heart, one of only two purely descriptive poems by Donne, it seems to be a dangerously thin straw to clutch at.

However, we can make some sensible approximations about the chronology of his work.

Most of his *Elegies* and the *Satyres* were composed during the 1590s, when he was either travelling and fighting abroad, or living the life of an intellectual rake at Lincoln's Inn. The Inns of Court were at this time the living quarters for a great number of aristocratic young men who had left university but were not studying law seriously. It was even referred to as the 'Third Universitie of England', but rather than pursuing any serious academic study, most of the wealthy young students put all their energies into revels and masques, and writing poetry, which was extremely fashionable. Although they might not have had the framework of a real university to control them, undoubtedly they did expend a great deal of time in intellectual pursuits, and Donne's *Satyre* I, 'On London Society', is itself a very intriguing glimpse into that life. Donne read widely in Spanish, Italian and French, and possessed an impressive library. Grierson notes that in 1623 he told the Duke of Buckingham he had more Spanish books on poetry or theology in his collection than in any other language, and they included the very latest works on theology.[2] To balance this picture of the intellectual young man, Grierson adds the frequently quoted comment made by Sir Richard Baker that Donne was, 'not dissolute but very neat: a great visiter of ladies, a great frequenter of plays, a great writer of conceited verses',[3] and what this leaves us with is probably a fairly believable sketch of the man. How long Donne travelled in Europe, precisely where, and how much contact he had with the large number of young Catholic Englishmen who had chosen exile for themselves, is impossible to know, but the Inns of Court were a major recruiting ground for Jesuits. It therefore seems fair to surmise that this period of his life, however hedonistic we might choose to see it, was also one filled with personal danger, as his brother Henry discovered. Amidst the plays, the poetry and the pleasure, was the real possibility of betrayal, imprisonment and death; and to assign solely those poems which smack of the former to this period would be unwise. Donne's adult mind, like any educated man of his age, was built on religious foundations, and his apostasy is every bit as real a crisis as his elopement, and both belong to this period, though how many poems do is entirely uncertain.

Donne's most famous work is the collection of poems called the *Songs and Sonnets*, and a firm date has not been agreed by critics for any of them. Grierson includes 55 poems in this group. However, *A Valediction: forbidding mourning* was dated by Walton to 1611, when Donne was 39, and *Twicknam Garden*, because of the date the Countess of Bedford took over the house, cannot really have been written before he was about the same age, so it appears sensible to assume with John Carey,[4] that Donne was writing them certainly beyond the Lincoln's Inn days, and may well have composed some of them much later.

The second great group of poems is referred to as the Divine Poems and this includes the *Holy Sonnets*, a group of 19 sonnets, most of which critics agree, were written around 1609–10; *La Corona*, a set of seven sonnets on the Crucifixion, dated 1607, and a number of individual poems which appear to belong to Donne's later years at St Paul's. These include *Good Friday, 1613. Riding Westward* and *A Hymne to God the Father*. It is equally erroneous to ascribe all of the Divine Poems to Donne's later years after ordination. As we have discovered, religious controversy and debate was something he inherited, and to counter the licentious picture he gives us of his associate in *Satyre* I, there is the energetic frustration and intense emotional involvement in faith of *Satyre* III.

Curiously, in applying the term 'metaphysics' to Donne, Dryden thought he was degrading him as a love poet. 'He affects the metaphysics, not only in his satires, but in his amorous verses, where nature only should reign; and perplexes the minds of the fair sex with nice speculations of philosophy, when he should engage their hearts, and entertain them with softness of love.'[5] In effect he put his critical finger on the absolute pulse which energises Donne's poetry. If we examine his use of the word, and so accepted is the term few critics ever do, Dryden seems to be criticising Donne's lack of naturalism. Donne's philosophising in all his poetry offended Dryden's sense of what poetry was for. His criticism of the love poetry is especially fascinating in view of contemporary feminist criticism which often lambasts Donne as an unmitigated misogynist. Even Dryden could see that the whole tenor of Donne's love poetry appealed to his reader's intellect. Where Donne is a seducer in his love poetry, at least he seduces minds and not vanity. He was more than capable of the latter, as his *Anniversaries* and poems to wealthy female patrons like the Countess of Huntingdon prove.

But what Dryden was actually noticing, as we have discovered repeatedly in our analyses, was that almost all of Donne's verse is driven by thought and not sensuality. If Donne used his experience it was to reflect on it, not recount it. If he addressed a lover or his God, he thought before he spoke.

Grierson also included 35 *Letters to Severall Personages*, a number of Epigrams, Epithalamions, lesser poems and Latin poems, as well as the unfinished lengthy poem, *Of the Progresse of the Soule*, which Donne began in 1601 while working for Egerton. This ambitious effort was a satirical epic which aimed to trace the progress of the apple plucked by Eve through to its final resting place in Donne's day. Two candidates have been brought to light by critical effort, Calvin or Queen Elizabeth, the latter a remarkably dangerous choice for a young Catholic man. However, only 52 verses survive, since Donne curtailed his efforts and never finished the poem. Critical opinion is strongly divided on its worth, so Donne's reputation as a poet today rests almost wholly on the *Songs and Sonnets* and the Divine Poems.

His prose works include *Pseudo-Martyr*, his emotional assault on Catholic martyrs; *Ignatius his Conclave*, a ferocious anti-Jesuit diatribe; and *Biathanatos*, his confused defence of suicide. Serious students of Donne might also seek out Essays in Divinity, Devotions, Sermons and Letters, all of which exist in modern editions.

9

The Critical History

In 1633, two years after his death, a small volume of Donne's poetry was printed and it was enough to take him out of the coterie he had been confined to all his adult life. Although in the subsequent years, his poetry was undervalued compared to Cowley's imitations of him, Donne influenced a number of poets sufficiently for the term 'Metaphysical school' to have arisen. But not until Coleridge championed him in the early eighteenth century, and later Browning, did his unique qualities begin to be fully appreciated. The Victorians also prized him for his prose, especially his sermons, but it was T.S. Eliot who, in the early years of the twentieth century, injected the critical impetus needed to push Donne to the front rank as an English poet. Sir Herbert Grierson published the first authoritative edition of Donne's entire poetical output in 1912, and it remains the definitive edition, although the steady rise in Donne's popularity has fuelled new editions and collections. In this chapter we will look at that critical history and bring it absolutely up to date.

We have already touched on Dryden in Chapter 8, but since he was the first to use the term 'Metaphysical' of Donne, we should examine his comments fully. In *A Discourse Concerning the Original and Progress of Satire*, 1693, Dryden praises the Earl of Dorset as 'equal Donne in the variety, multiplicity, and choice of thoughts', and goes on to say he excels him in the actual business of writing poetry, criticising Donne as we have seen, for 'He affects the metaphysics, not only in his satires, but in his amorous verses, where nature only should reign; and perplexes the minds of the fair sex

174

with nice speculations of philosophy, when he should engage their hearts, and entertain them with the softnesses of love.'[1] The work done in Part I of this book should be enough to have shown how Dryden's view is encumbered by his sense of what poetry, especially love poetry, should be. We have seen how Donne's love poetry, though frequently addressed to 'the fair sex', is not even interested in the conventional modes of address, and opts instead for more subtle ways to praise or seduce. Dryden appears to assume that the female mind is capable of only one form of address, flattery. If Donne flatters his female reader, it is through the pleasure of keeping up with his wit. It would be absurd to suggest that Donne possessed a post-feminist mentality in this, but it is equally absurd to criticise him, as some contemporary feminist critics have, for not possessing one. Donne inhabited a nominally patriarchal society (though ironically even that is not strictly true, since Elizabeth I was a woman and one with divine right), and to criticise his imagery or wit for appealing to male taste or masculine values is a poorly disguised attempt to control that taste and reshape those values.

Dryden's second attack on Donne is also revealing and helps us to appreciate why Donne earned such a high reputation amongst his contemporaries as an original. Dryden adds, 'Would not Donne's *Satyres*, which abound with so much wit, appear more charming, if he had taken care of his words, and of his numbers?' I hope we have seen enough in Part 1 of Donne's satire to recognise 'charming' is not something it ever aspires to be, but we should also note here that Dryden felt Donne's metrical skill to be lacking. We have seen how, in Donne, rhythm is repeatedly governed by sense, and how confidently and often surprisingly he manipulates it. Frustration, anger, emotional outbursts, imperatives, pepper his verse. Time and time again poems open with an assertiveness it is difficult to resist, a fierce need to be heard. What Dryden wanted was something more like Donne's contemporaries were used to, a harmony and predictability which was essentially more lyrical and courteous. As an example, here is a sonnet by Sir Philip Sydney, the perfect scholar, gentleman and soldier of the Elizabethan period. In his sequence of sonnets, *Astrophil and Stella*, he described a fictional version of his relationship with Penelope Devereux. This is the first of them.

Astrophil and Stella Sonnet 1

Loving in truth, and fain in verse my love to show,
That she (dear she) might take some pleasure of my pain:
Pleasure might cause her read, reading might make her know,
Knowledge might pity win, and pity grace obtain,
    I sought fit words to paint the blackest face of woe,
Studying inventions fine, her wits to entertain:
Oft turning others' leaves, to see if thence would flow
Some fresh and fruitful showers upon my sun-burn'd brain.
    But words came halting forth, wanting Invention's stay,
Invention Nature's child, fled step-dame Study's blows,
And others' feet still seem'd but strangers in my way.
Thus great with child to speak, and helpless in my throes,
    Biting my truand pen, beating myself for spite,
    Fool, said my Muse to me, look in thy heart and write.

It is not difficult to see how different this is to Donne's sonnets. The rhythm is liltingly obvious; the courtesy glaringly evident in the parenthesis '(dear she)' and the ideas linked logically and simply by parataxis, the step-by-step connecting of ideas as in a chain. Donne's rhythm is never as smooth, and, as we discovered in our analyses, the difficulty often the result of ellipsis and hypotaxis, the linking of ideas in subordination. Sidney's sonnet, as a piece of love poetry, though technically adept, is insipid when placed against the coruscations of wit and emotion Donne displays. Were we to carry out the kind of detailed analysis practised in Part I on the Sidney sonnet, it would be extremely revealing. But as a gesture in that direction, look closely at Sidney's concluding couplet. What we are given is a picture of the pen-nibbling poet, frustratedly struggling to find the words to express his love, and deciding, as though in a moment of inspiration ('said my Muse to me') that he need only seek in his heart for the words, as though this declaration will in itself speak volumes. Ironically Donne make us feel he does precisely what Sidney admits he cannot. Sidney's admission of his own artifice undermines the poem's sincerity so completely, that the final couplet's attempt to salvage it merely stresses the failing. In Donne we not only get the impression he has already looked in his heart, but his intestines as well, and for some considerable time before ever setting pen to paper.

Dr Johnson, the great lexicographer and critic of the eighteenth century, was the next major figure to contribute to the development of Donne's poetic reputation. Writing in his *Lives of the Poets*, 1779, he maintained that

> The metaphysical poets were men of learning, and to show their
> learning was their whole endeavour; but, unluckily resolving to show
> it in rhyme, instead of writing poetry they only wrote verses, and very
> often such verses as stood the trial of the finger better than of the ear;
> for the modulation was so imperfect, that they were only to be found
> verses by counting the syllables.[2]

Like Dryden, Johnson dislikes Donne for something he never attempts: the conventional lyricism of writers like Sidney. Johnson appears to use 'modulation' as a synonym for rhythm, and is seeking above all harmony and balance, something more akin to music than Donne was usually interested in. He continues with his age's ingrained respect for classical thought, as follows:

> If the father of criticism has rightly been denominated poetry, . . . an
> imitative art, these writers will, without great wrong, lose their right to
> the name of poets, for they cannot be said to have imitated anything;
> they neither copied nature nor life, neither painted the forms of
> matter, nor represented the operations of the intellect.
>
> Those, however, who deny them to be poets, allow them to be wits.
> Dryden confesses of himself and his contemporaries, that they fall
> below Donne in wit, but maintains that they surpass him in poetry.
>
> If wit be well described by Pope, as being 'that which has been
> often thought, but was never before so well expressed,' they certainly
> never attained, nor ever sought it; for they endeavoured to be singular
> in their thoughts, and were careless of their diction. But Pope's
> account of wit is undoubtedly erroneous: he depresses it below its
> natural dignity, and reduces it from strength of thought to happiness
> of language.
>
> If by a more noble and more adequate conception that be consid-
> ered wit which is at once natural and new, that which, though not
> obvious, is, upon its first production, acknowledged to be just; if it be

that which he that never found it wonders how he missed, to wit of this kind the metaphysical poets have seldom risen. Their thoughts are often new, but seldom natural; they are not obvious, but neither are they just; and the reader, far from wondering that he missed them, wonders more frequently by what perverseness of industry they were ever found.

But wit, abstracted from its effects upon the hearer, may be more rigorously and philosophically considered as a kind of *discordia concors*; a combination of dissimilar images, or discovery of occult resemblances in things apparently unlike. Of wit, thus defined, they have more than enough. The most heterogeneous ideas are yoked by violence together; nature and art are ransacked for illustrations, comparisons, and allusions; their learning instructs, and their subtlety surprises; but the reader commonly thinks his improvement dearly bought, and, though he sometimes admires, is seldom pleased.

From this account of their compositions it will be readily inferred that they were not successful in representing or moving the affections.

As they were wholly employed on something unexpected and surprising, they had no regard to that kind of uniformity of sentiment which enables us to conceive and to excite the pains and the pleasure of other minds: they never inquired what, on any occasion, they should have said or done, but wrote rather as beholders than partakers of human nature; as beings looking upon good and evil, impassive and at leisure; as Epicurean deities, making remarks on the actions of men, and the vicissitudes of life, without interest and without emotion. Their courtship was void of fondness, and their lamentation of sorrow. Their wish was only to say what they hoped had never been said before.

Nor was the sublime more within their reach than the pathetic; for they never attempted that comprehension and expanse of thought which at once fills the whole mind, and of which the first effect is sudden astonishment, and the second rational admiration. Sublimity is produced by aggregation, and littleness by dispersion. Great thoughts are always general, and consist in positions not limited by exceptions, and in descriptions not descending to minuteness. It is with great propriety that subtlety, which in its original import means exility of particles, is taken in its metaphorical meaning for nicety of distinction. Those writers who lay on the watch for novelty could have little hope of greatness; for great things cannot have escaped former observation. Their attempts were always analytic; they broke every image into fragments; and could no more represent, by their slender conceits and laboured particularities, the prospects of nature, or the scenes of life, than he who dissects a sunbeam with a prism can exhibit the wide effulgence of a summer noon.

What they wanted however of the sublime, they endeavoured to supply by hyperbole; their amplification had no limits; they left not only reason but fancy behind them; and produced combinations of confused magnificence, that not only could not be credited, but could not be imagined.

Yet great labour, directed by great abilities, is never wholly lost; if they frequently threw away their wit upon false conceits, they likewise sometimes struck out an unexpected truth; if their conceits were far-fetched, they were often worth the carriage. To write on their plan, it was at least necessary to read and think. No man could be born a metaphysical poet, nor assume the dignity of a writer, by descriptions copied from descriptions, by imitations borrowed from imitations, by traditional imagery, and hereditary similes, by readiness of rhyme, and volubility of syllables.

In perusing the works of this race of authors, the mind is exercised either by recollection or inquiry; either something already learned is to be retrieved, or something new is to be examined. If their greatness seldom elevates, their acuteness often surprises; if the imagination is not always gratified, at least the powers of reflection and comparison are employed; and in the mass of materials which ingenious absurdity has thrown together, genuine wit and useful knowledge may some-times be found buried perhaps in grossness of expression, but useful to those who know their value; and such as, when they are expanded to perspicuity, and polished to elegance, may give lustre to works which have more propriety though less copiousness of sentiment.[3]

Johnson goes on to cite Donne as the former amongst these unfortunately restricted minds. Johnson's view was very influential and has been quoted at length because of that. Yet what he succeeded in doing was not quite what he intended, and by attacking them for their limitations, he ended up encouraging other poets to respond to their obviously creative gifts. Armed with our knowledge of Donne from the practical analyses of Part I, we are in a position now to evaluate some of Johnson's comments.

Using Aristotle as his unassailable proof, he starts by denying

Donne's right to the title of poet at all, since he was not capable of mimicking nature or life. We have seen how disinterested Donne is in purely descriptive writing, and how the potential of language and thought are his real preoccupations. Yet Johnson specifically denies him the latter too, 'nor represented the operations of the intellect'. As though aware that this is a difficult claim, he proceeds to temper it somewhat by a digression into the meaning of wit and whether or not the Metaphysicals possessed any. Johnson is quite right to correct Pope's purely linguistic definition of wit and make of it something more intellectual. But is he right in his insistence that Donne's 'thoughts are often new, but seldom natural; they are not obvious, but neither are they just'? Perhaps what Johnson really meant by 'natural' and 'just' was conventional, ideas the reader recognises as potentially his own. If so, we can see why Donne could not possibly satisfy him. He was far too embroiled in his own thoughts, products of his lived experience as lover and apostate, to worry about what others were thinking.

The great critical interest and energy expended in more recent years on Donne's biographical details may well reflect Johnson's assertion that the reader's response to his thoughts is more usually not that, 'he missed them', but, 'more frequently by what perverseness of industry they were ever found'. A modern response is far more likely to be a pyschological one which makes us question what aspect of the real man's real life could have engendered them.

Seeking further insight in his criticism, Johnson then refines his definition of wit even further, but in his use of the Latin *discordia concors*; 'a combination of dissimilar images, or discovery of occult resemblances in things apparently unlike', he is doing little more than resorting to metaphor as his ideal form. (For Johnson 'occult' merely meant hidden and had none of the modern connotations of magic.) It is this portion of the essay which gave rise to the phrase which came to typify the practice of Metaphysical poetry, and Donne in particular. 'The most heterogeneous ideas are yoked by violence together; nature and art are ransacked for illustrations, comparisons, and allusions'; but the confident conclusion he draws from it should surprise us, 'it will be readily inferred that they were not successful in representing or moving the affections'.

We should be similarly surprised by his subsequent description of Donne and his like as, 'Epicurean deities, making remarks on the actions of men, and the vicissitudes of life, without interest and without emotion', and his attack on Donne's lacking sublimity is difficult to justify when placed against our description of him as one of the few English poets who writes about his spiritual health. However, his reference to hyperbole is something that should come as no surprise whatsoever, and his comment that they, 'produced combinations of confused magnificence, that not only could not be credited, but could not be imagined', may say more about Johnson as a reader than Donne as a poet. Ironically this parting shot so struck home that Donne's reputation today as a writer and thinker far outweighs Johnson's. In praising the occasional spark of real wit and intellect hidden 'in grossness of expression', he imagined that future writers might be able to make better use of them than Donne, 'when they are expanded to perspicuity, and polished to elegance, may give lustre to works which have more propriety though less copiousness of sentiment', and indeed it was largely the praise of other poets – Coleridge, Browning and T.S. Eliot among them – that fuelled Donne's reputational rise. Thomas de Quincey voiced some of these objections to Johnson's criticism more than volubly when he wrote:

> Few writers have shown a more extraordinary compass of powers than Donne; for he combined what no other man has ever done – the least sublimation of dialectical subtlety and address with the most impassioned majesty. . . . No criticism was ever more unhappy than that of Dr Johnson's, which denounces all this artificial display as so much perversion of taste.'[4]

We have already touched on some of Coleridge's ideas about Donne in Chapter 6, and his admiration of his predecessor led him to make some useful observations. 'To read Dryden, Pope, &c., you need only count syllables; but to read Donne you must measure *Time*, and discover the *Time* of each word by the sense of Passion.'[5] What Coleridge had noticed was precisely what Dr Johnson decried, Donne's habitual tendency to sublimate sense or feeling above formal metre. Coleridge's words and emphases show how difficult he found it to articulate his idea, but in a cultural climate where children are routinely taught that creativity should not be shackled by anything as tedious as grammar or spelling, we should have less difficulty:

> Doubtless, all the copies I have ever seen of Donne's poems are grievously misprinted. Wonderful that they are not more so, considering that not one in a thousand of his readers have any notion how his lines are to be read – to the many, five out of six appear anti-metrical. How greatly this aided the compositor's negligence or ignorance, and prevented the corrector's remedy, any man may ascertain by examining the earliest editions of blank verse plays, Massinger, Beaumont and Fletcher, &c. Now, Donne's rhythm was as inexplicable to the many as blank verse, spite of his rhymes – *ergo*, as blank verse misprinted. I am convinced that where no mode of rational declamation by pause, hurrying of voice, or apt and sometimes double emphasis, can at once make the verse metrical and bring out the sense of passion more prominently, there we are entitled to alter the text, when it can be done by simple omission or addition of *that*, *which*, *and*, and such 'small deer'; or by mere new placing of the same words – I would venture nothing beyond.

> And by delighting many, frees again
> Grief which Verse did restrain.
>
> > *The Triple Fool*, v. 15

A good instance of how Donne read his own verses. We should write 'The Grief, verse did restrain;' but Donne roughly emphasised the two words, Grief and Verse, and, therefore, made each the first syllable of a trochee or dactyll:

> Grief, which | verse did re | strain.

> What ever dies is not mixt equally;
> If our two loves be one, both thou and I
> Love just alike in all; none of these loves can die.
>
> > *The Good Morrow*

Too good for mere wit. It contains a deep practical truth, this triplet.

To Canonization

One of my favourite poems. As late as ten years ago, I used to seek and find out grand lines and fine stanzas; but my delight has been far greater since it has consisted in tracing the leading thought thro'ghout the whole. The former is too much like coveting your neighbour's goods; in the latter you merge yourself with the author, you *become He*.

To a Valediction: forbidding mourning

An admirable poem which none but Donne could have written. Nothing was ever more admirably made out than the figure of the compass.[6]

Coleridge's admiration for Donne is transparent and his attempts to illustrate how to read him helpful, if a little technical for modern eyes. His point about the untrustworthy nature of editions of Donne is made clear when we compare the version of the triplet of *The Good-Morrow* he had with our version:

> What ever dyes, was not mixt equally;
> If our two loves be one, or, thou and I
> Love so alike, that none doe slacken, none can die.
>
> (*The Good Morrow*, ll. 19–21)

The next major figure to influence critical thinking on Donne, if we exclude the publication of Grierson's *Poetical Works* , was the poet T.S. Eliot, and predominantly in an essay called 'The Metaphysical Poets' published in 1921. After praising Grierson for his work, Eliot stresses the difficulty in defining Metaphysical poetry and in deciding who is a Metaphysical poet, and asks whether they form a school, or movement of writers in any meaningful sense:

> It is difficult to find any precise use of metaphor, simile or other conceit, which is common to all the poets and at the same time important enough as an element of style to isolate these poets as a group. Donne, and often Cowley, employ a device which is some-times considered characteristically 'metaphysical'; the elaboration (contrasted and with the condensation) of a figure of speech to the

furthest stage to which ingenuity can carry it. Thus Cowley develops
the commonplace comparison of the world to a chess-board through
long stanzas (*To Destiny*), and Donne, with more grace, in *A
Valediction*, the comparison of two lovers to a pair of compasses. But
elsewhere we find, instead of the mere explication of the content of a
comparison, a development by rapid association of thought which
requires considerable agility on the part of the reader:

> *On a round ball*
> *A workeman that hath copies by, can lay*
> *An Europe, Afrique, and an Asia,*
> *And quickly make that, which was nothing, All,*
> > *So doth each teare,*
> > *Which thee doth weare,*
> *A globe, yea world by that impression grow,*
> *Till thy tears mixt with mine doe overflow*
> *This world, by waters sent from thee, my heaven dissolved so.*

Here we find at least two connexions which are not implicit in the
first figure, but are forced upon it by the poet: from the geographer's
globe to the tear, and the tear to the deluge. On the other hand some
of Donne's most successful and characteristic effects are secured by
brief words and sudden contrasts.

> *A bracelet of bright hair about the bone,*

where the most powerful effect is produced by the sudden contrast of
associations of 'bright hair' and 'bone'. This telescoping of images and
multiplied associations is characteristic of the phrase of some of the
dramatists of the period which Donne knew: not to mention
Shakespeare, it is frequent in Middleton, Webster, and Tourner, and
is one of the sources of the vitality of their language. . . .

It is certain that the dramatic verse of the later Elizabethan and
early Jacobean poets expresses a degree of development of sensibility
which is not found in any of the prose, good as it often is. If we except
Marlowe, a man of prodigious intelligence, these dramatists were
directly or indirectly (it is at least a tenable theory) affected by
Montaigne. Even if we except also Jonson and Chapman, these two
were notably erudite, and were notably men who incorporated their
erudition into their sensibility: their mode of feeling was directly and

freshly altered by their reading and thought. In Chapman especially there is a direct sensuous apprehension of thought, or a recreation of thought into feeling, which is exactly what we find in Donne:

> *in this one thing, all the discipline*
> *Of manners and of manhood is contained;*
> *A man to join himself with th'Universe*
> *In his main sway, and make in all things fit*
> *One with that All, and go on, round as it;*
> *Not plucking from the whole his wretched part,*
> *And into straits, or into nought revert,*
> *Wishing the complete Universe might be*
> *Subject to such a rag of it as he;*
> *But to consider great Necessity.*

We compare this with some modern passage:

> *No, when the fight begins within himself,*
> *A man's worth something. God stoops o'er his head,*
> *Satan looks up between his feet – both tug -*
> *He's left, himself, i'the middle; the soul wakes*
> *And grows. Prolong that battle through his life!*

It is perhaps somewhat less fair, though very tempting (as both poets are concerned with the perpetuation of love by offspring), to compare with the stanzas already quoted from Lord Herbert's Ode the following from Tennyson:

> *One walked between his wife and child,*
> *With measured footfall firm and mild,*
> *And now and then he gravely smiled.*
>   *The prudent partner of his blood*
>   *Leaned on him, faithful, gentle, good,*
> *And in their double love secure,*
> *The little maiden walked demure,*
> *Pacing with downward eyelids pure.*
>   *These three made unity so sweet,*
> *My frozen heart began to beat,*
>   *Remembering its ancient heat.*

The difference is not a simple difference of degree between poets. It is something which had happened to the mind of England between the time of Donne or Lord Herbert of Cherbury and the time of Tennyson and Browning; it is the difference between the intellectual poet and the reflective poet. Tennyson and Browning are poets, and they think; but they do not feel their thought as immediately as the odour of a rose. A thought to Donne was an experience; it modified his sensibility. When a poet's mind is perfectly equipped for its work, it is constantly amalgamating disparate experience; the ordinary man's experience is chaotic, irregular, fragmentary. The latter falls in love, or reads Spinoza, and these two experiences have nothing to do with each other, or with the noise of the typewriter or the smell of cooking; in the mind of the poet these experiences are always forming new wholes.[7]

Eliot then proceeds to enunciate the theory that Donne and his ilk were genuine successors to the poets of the previous century and 'possessed a mechanism of sensibility which could devour any kind of experience.' But in the seventeenth century he argues, a 'dissociation of sensibility set in, from which we have never recovered', a dissociation he lays firmly at the door of Milton and Dryden. These two, 'performed certain poetic functions so magnificently well that the magnitude of the effect concealed the absence of others', and although the language continued to develop, and 'became more refined, the feeling became more crude.' He continues the essay as follows:

After this brief exposition of a theory – too brief, perhaps, to carry conviction – we may ask, what would have been the fate of the 'metaphysical' had the current of poetry descended in a direct line from them, as it descended in a direct line to them? They would not, certainly, be classified as metaphysical. The possible interests of a poet are unlimited; the more intelligent he is the better; the more intelligent he is the more likely that he will have interests: our only condition is that he turn them into poetry, and not merely meditate on them poetically. A philosophical theory which has entered into poetry is established, for its truth or falsity in one sense ceases to matter, and its truth in another sense is proved. The poets in question have, like other poets, various faults. But they were, at best, engaged in the task of trying to find the verbal equivalent for states of mind and feeling. And this means both that they are more mature, and that they wear better, than later poets of certainly not less literary ability.[8]

Eliot's isolation of two aspects of Cowley and Donne's verse, the elaborate conceit, ingeniously stretched, and the leap by association from one idea to another which exercises the reader's own imaginative capacity, were taken up widely in the study and teaching of Donne. Eliot links this with the infamously vital and energetic dramatists of the period, and from there he uses examples to suggest that between Donne and the Victorians, Tennyson and Browning, 'something had happened to the mind of England', and that something he describes as the shift from the poetry of intellect to the poetry of reflection. It allows him to make one of the most incisive critical observations ever written about Donne, 'A thought to Donne was an experience; it modified his sensibility.'

What Eliot attempts is a way of defining the nature of a poet by using Donne. Whereas the ordinary man simply wallows in experience, however erudite, the poet synthesises even the most heterogeneous of experiences – reading Spinoza or cooking – and from this synthesis creates poetry. Not surprisingly, then, Eliot views intelligence as an absolute prerequisite for a poet, since the intelligent man is likely to have more interests. Although our age would eagerly cheer on his ready acceptance that, 'the possible interests of a poet are unlimited', it is more interesting to ponder how readily it would accept his former assertion that the poet must be an intelligent man. As some critics have suggested, there is a lot of Eliot himself in this image of the poet, but that does not undermine his insights on Donne at all. We have seen in our analyses how skilfully Donne unites disparate ideas and connects widely divergent topics; how eclectic is his search for material, and how redolent of his own personality is his own verse. Eliot might not entirely succeed in answering the question he set himself at the start of the essay, but he did tease out some of Donne's most elusive characteristics, and opened the way for others to build on his insights and explore Donne's use of conceit more thoroughly.

Since Eliot showed the route, many excellent critical minds have further enhanced Donne's reputation as a poet and sieved from what history has left us an increasingly helpful body of knowledge about his poetic style and life. The effect has been gradually to isolate him from the Metaphysical Poets as a group, or indeed to use his uniqueness to deflate the value of the others, and it is far more likely today that a student will study Donne alone than the Metaphysical Poets as a movement. There is not room to summarise all their efforts, but many of these critics are mentioned in the Further Reading section at the end of this book.

To complete this study, the final chapter will concentrate on the most up-to-date critical work on Donne, giving us the opportunity to consider a number different opinions in the light of our own analyses, the suggested work we may have completed, and our knowledge of the critical history which has brought us to this point.

10

Contemporary Critical Views

In any critical overview of recent work on Donne, it would be impossible to ignore John Carey's provocative book, *John Donne: Life, Mind and Art*, which draws heavily on history, biographical material and psychology to explore Donne's mind. In it he uses paradox and Donne's love of it to reconcile the two traditional faces of the poet: love poet and religious supplicant. Carey offers some detailed analyses of a number of key poems and continually provides stimulating observations, but they tend to be overwhelmed by his handling of Donne's life and interests which combine to create the impression that the study is more interested in the poet than the poetry. Yet it has to be said that readers of Donne commonly find themselves drawn into a fascination with their sense of the poet's identity which the poetry itself stimulates, and so Carey's emphasis is in a way not surprising at all.

In detailing the historical background and specific events which shaped Donne's early life, his Catholic upbringing, education and ambitious drive, Carey settles on his apostasy as the single most powerful fact we need to know in studying his poetry. 'The first thing to remember about Donne is that he was a Catholic; the second, that he betrayed his faith.'[1] The poetic evidence for this he cites as *Satyre* III which he calls, 'the great, crucial poem of Donne's early manhood'.[2] He analyses the emotional tone of the poem, but is most interested in the way the poem skirts around Catholicism's claim to be the one true faith. In referring to 'thy father's spirit', Carey explores the idea that the poem actually embodies the intellectual struggle it attempts to discuss:

it's hard to believe that in Satire III, when Donne writes about religion and fathers, he does so without any thought of his own father, whose religion he is about to abandon. His father had been a Catholic, and the 'easie ways and near' he taught were those of Rome. Since he assumes that his father is in heaven, and since Satire III is adamant that there is only one true religion which leads to heaven, the argument of the poem would appear to be over before it has begun. There is no need to start labouring up Truth's hill; Catholicism must be right. Viewed in this way, the contrast between the part of the poem which springs from Donne's deeper emotional loyalties, and the part directed by his brave new investigative spirit, becomes sharper . . . Only in the oblique and uncertain allusion to his dead father do we get any hint of the kind of inner attachment Donne found himself struggling against. There is no other mention of family or friends. The poem's effort is to make out that choosing a religion is purely an intellectual business, as unemotional as mountaineering. Donne needed to convince himself of this, in order to allay his personal turmoil. So the Satire is not an account of a crisis but an operative part of one. It was, for its author, a necessary poem, and its inconsistency and misrepresentation are part of its vigorous life.[3]

Carey's emphasis on Donne's apostasy has engendered criticism in its turn. Dennis Flynn's essay, 'Donne the Survivor',[4] attacks Carey's use of the term 'apostasy' as a departure from earlier criticism and 'a dead metaphor. . . . To be consistent,' Flynn argues, 'he should have avoided the ironical, dead metaphor *apostasy* and dealt in phenomena and concepts more available to our common usage in this pluralist world.

'I propose instead that we describe Donne not as an "apostate" or as a "blasphemer" but simply as a "survivor" of the Elizabethan persecution.' Flynn then tries to connect the persecution of the Catholics under Elizabeth and the persecution of Jews in our own century, in order for him to employ the ideas of the writer Bruno Bettleheim, in an essay entitled 'Trauma and Reintegration', to stress Donne's feelings of guilt at having survived.

Apart from Flynn's flagrant willingness to accept contemporary cultural ignorance as a reason for adopting new terminologies, his argument relies on forcing the link between Elizabeth's England and Nazi Germany, and making Donne a victim of trauma. We might encourage some more precise thought on all of this if we compare Donne to the position of a fictional Jew in Nazi Germany who not only actively encourages, by his writings, the continued persecution of his fellow Jews, but who wholly abandons his religious faith for that of his political masters. That analogy makes 'survivor' a difficult term to swallow. But perhaps the soundest comment on Donne's apostasy comes, not surprisingly, from Grierson where he writes with acute simplicity, 'Donne would not have become a Protestant in a Catholic country'.[5] Carey's additional point about the inconsistency and misrepresentation in *Satyre* III, is one he expands on throughout the book, but especially in chapter 6, 'Change'. Analysing *The Apparition*, and eschewing comparisons of it to Petrarchan poems, Carey writes:

'The Apparition' is wholly different though, not only because of its drama and wit, but also because of its inconsistency. At the start Donne is professedly dying of unrequited love; yet at the end he tells the girl that he is out of love, and would rather she suffered, after his death, than that she should grant him her love and save his life. How can he be dying of love, and out of love? Does he love her, or doesn't he? Does he pretend he's still in love, and dying of it to make her ashamed? Or to justify his hatred, which he can do only by making out that she has damaged him irreparably? Or is he really still in love with her ; and does he say he's not because he's in a rage and wants to pay her out? Or because, being the cruellest thing he can say, it might just frighten her into loving him in return? These different possibilities don't exhaust the alternatives that the poem suggests, but they're enough to indicate the confused motives underlying it.

Further, the poem doesn't sort them out into alternatives. It implies them all at once, reminding us that only in a simplified account of the human psyche do contradictory feelings like love and hate have to be regarded as contradictory. . . . Even in death Donne can't imagine not pursuing the girl. There's no telling whether the poem's scabrous, clever tone is adopted as a weapon to hurt her, or as a shield to hide his own incoherent feelings. Sarcasm and jocularity serve either purpose, or both, in life, and our not being able to guess which is uppermost is no more than we should expect from our daily observation.

Though 'The Apparition' is an extreme example, it is not singular.

Complexity of attitude is the usual thing in Donne, and usually arises from changes or contradictions within the poem. The complexities are not riddles to be solved, but natural and unresolvable, like living. They keep us at bay, as people do, and, as with people, there is no chance of cracking them open to find clear meanings inside. We have to surmise, and have nothing to go on but our own experience. Trying to understand them, we're obliged to think our way down into our own divisive impulses, and that makes the poems educative.[6]

Carey's point that the poems are not riddles to be solved is especially pertinent in view of the tendency of critics to pursue doggedly the biographical root of the poems. Indeed it is something Carey himself is criticised for. Roger B. Rollin, in his essay, '"FANTASTIQUE AGUE" The Holy Sonnets and Religious Melancholy',[7] describes Carey as a 'psychobiographical critic' for his reading of, 'the Holy Sonnets as if each poem were a versified treatment of an actual event in Donne's psychological life'.

Carey expands his view of Donne's essentially human and therefore ultimately mysterious poetry in his chapter 'The Crisis of Reason'. Considering the function of reason in Donne he writes:

This is worth doing, because the force of his reasoning is evidently one thing that makes his poetry distinctive. He is – in J.B. Leishman's phrase – 'an argumentative poet'. But immediately we apply that label we see how misleading it is. Someone who had never read Donne would get quite the wrong impression from it. An argumentative poet, he would assume, marshals evidence and reaches conclusions. Donne does not. His arguments are frivolous, tenuous or self-contradictory by turns, but they are almost never genuinely argumentative. He treats argument not as an instrument for discovering truth but as a flexible poetic accessory, like rhyme or alliteration. It is an agitated facade through which he projects the desires and inconstancies of his poetic self. We are not at all surprised to find him turning round and disparaging the arguments he has fabricated, as in 'Womans Constancy':

> Vaine lunatique, against these scapes I could
> Dispute, and conquer, if I would.

Argument, he impresses on us, is at the service of the will. Logic is a convenient and adaptable screen for appetite. Given sufficient incentive, he will reason his way in or out of any position.[8]

To conclude his study, Carey draws together his views under a chapter headed 'Imagined Corners', in which he takes a number of Donne's favourite words: angels, mummy, mandrakes, maps, coins and shadows and ingeniously decides they have one thing in common, 'they are meeting places for opposites.'[9] He then explores their essentially paradoxical qualities, that they are objects dragged apart from the normal, natural world by their peculiarly dual natures, and via a use of T.S. Eliot, shows how this fascination of Donne's was even more widespread than his initial, brief list indicates. This drive to unite and weld together essentially antipathetic things, he traces through many of Donne's greatest poems and celebrated images, ultimately finding its expression in his way of comprehending birth and death, and the union of body and soul itself. These things, Carey argues, excited Donne's imagination and animated his verse, because they appealed to a mind which history, family and fate had honed to dualise and synthesise habitually. In Carey's view, Donne's verse emanates from the man, and understanding the man allows us richer access to the verse.

Very different from Carey's more traditional approach is John Stachniewski's book, *The Persecutory Imagination*.[10] Stachniewski draws on post-structuralist and new historicist thinking, and particularly gains inspiration from Stephen Greenblatt's idea of an 'anthropological' criticism in his book, *Renaissance Self-Fashioning*,[11] where Greenblatt argues that: 'anthropological interpretation must address itself less to the mechanics of customs and institutions than to the interpretive constructions the members of a society apply to their experiences'.[12] Stachniewski's aim is simply to understand the way writers understood their own age, through their writing. Literature gives us a particularly strong ability to do this, since it generally concentrates on representing lived experience, whether real or fictional, and so embodies the way the men themselves viewed their age. While aware that literature allows us to see how men *felt* about what was happening to them, rather than what actually *was* happening, and that it is impossible to think outside of the linguistic framework which his own era imposes on him, he nonethelesss believes it possible to achieve this kind of a reading.

Unusually conscious of the pitfalls of post-structuralist criticism of various forms, where reforming fervour frequently crushes any pretence to objectivity, Stachniewski disclaims any desire for objectivity in favour of a methodology which is neither tainted by any particular critical dogma, nor a slave to canonical pressure. He believes himself reasonably capable of moving between the past and the present without being eager to alter the former in 'ways that suit our own preferred values'.[13] In summary, Stachniewski envisages criticism as a kind of anthropology where we can see into the lives of the past. Although he stresses he knows that his own use of language is tainted by the present, he has no cultural axe to grind beyond a 'naive intellectual curiosity: how, socially and psychologically, did people live with these ideas?'[14]

In Part I of his book he discusses Calvinism in relation to other Christian beliefs of the period, explaining clearly how it differs in its handling of predestination. Calvin, he argues, placed his followers in a peculiar spiritual dilemma arising from his notion that not only has God pre-ordained who will be saved, but there is nothing we can do to alter that. Faced with this terrible fear of not knowing if one is saved or not, Calvin's answer, when challenged, was supremely elusive: 'If Pighius asks how I know I am elect, I answer that Christ is more than a thousand testimonies to me.'[15] Noting that it was Calvin who gave us the word 'reprobate' to mean 'rejected by God', and that he imagined the experience of the reprobate as merely a sampler of hell, Stachniewski suggests that not only did these ideas generate despair amongst adherents, but that it was a well-recognised and widespread phenomenon in England from the early sixteenth century. Indeed Catholics used despair as something of a stick to beat Protestantism with precisely because of this. So powerful was this movement towards despair in early seventeenth-century England, that it was felt suicide had reached epidemic levels. Of course Calvin also viewed suicides as reprobates. Having established that Protestant despair was not only widespread, he then asserts it was virtually unavoidable by thinking Protestants. 'Religious despair was not, in origin at least, a psychological disorder (although it is revealing that people increasingly thought it was). It was a rational response to unchallengeable tenets – a product far more of nurture than of nature.'[16]

Social and economic circumstances contributed to the mood of despair, and Stachniewski suggests that the period of transition from a predominantly agragrian to an industrial society was the most fertile breeding ground for Calvinist thinking because it attached itself to the insecurity people felt. The unprecedently fluid society, where people were often the victims of movement, made predestination an agreeable explanation. At this point in his argument, Stachniewski makes a simple point which merits underscoring in view of many comments serious students of Donne will encounter in their reading. 'In the sixteenth and seventeenth centuries belief in God was not voluntary.'[17] People saw a personality at work behind the social and economic pressures they blossomed or wilted under. In literature we see the rise of rogue figures or malcontents, such as those in Webster's plays, and Puritans begin to try and assist men in their change from a feudal to industrial society. A final effect of the dominance of Calvinism was the reinforcement of patriarchal authority, and Stachniewski connects Calvin's terrifying God with the feared father of the family. Calvin actually stipulated the death penalty for parental disobedience, and although this was never made law in Geneva, it was the law in Connecticut and Massachusetts in the 1640s.

Having outlined very clearly the mood of the age, Stachniewski is then able to analyse Donne's *Holy Sonnets* and explore their mood of Protestant despair which contrasts directly with earlier views of the sonnets as constituting a sequence that moves towards peace of mind. For Stachniewski they are 'discrete *cris de coeur*'.[18] He explicitly criticises Helen Gardner's analysis of the sonnets, deciding her 'introduction of the Ignatian meditation to the discussion of the "Holy Sonnets" is, above all, redundant'.[19] He then notes how Donne's treatment as a Protestant writer has been entirely overshadowed by Milton's, yet the level of Protestant feeling and thought in Donne far exceeds that to be found in Milton.

The following extract gives a clearer taste of Stachniewski's response to the *Holy Sonnets* as disparate poems rather than a sequence:

> If it is assumed that Donne wrote poems about spiritual conflict from a pious and assured position, the 'Holy Sonnets' will not trouble other assumptions about the kind of God he believed in or about the responses this God evoked. That the writing wrestles with the oppressiveness of the collectively imagined deity and accompanying values can be, and with amazing success has been, rendered invisible. Arguments for sequence have helped to achieve this since the impact and meaning of individual poems in a sequence which plots a thematic development is controlled and restricted by the overall artistic design to which they contribute. A sonnet occupying a position in this sequence sacrifices the emotional complexity which thrives on the brevity of the dramatic lyric to a unifying idea and attitude over which the artist exercises purposeful control. Few critics of the 'Holy Sonnets' would wish to dissent from the view of William Halewood (another critic who sees the poems as Augustinian meditations) that they were written 'within a secure framework of belief' and 'that they were written according to a formula that could produce only "poetry of exclusion" – to recur again to Richard's term for poetry which commits itself to the suppression of emotional ambiguities.' If, however, the poems are read as independent articulations in which the discipline of tight verse form is bought to bear on an often disturbed psychic state, emotional ambiguities will, on the contrary, constitute their vital meaning.[20]

He then applies his thinking consistently to several of the sonnets and his analysis of *Sonnet X* follows:

> In the 'Holy Sonnets' the manipulation of mood is particularly unavailing since he is confronting what he sees as the ultimate reality of his position. Self-bamboozlement is worse than useless. The poem's meaning lives in the tension between the argument and the emotion and this tension tends to make us aware that the despairing sonnets are not , as they may at first appear, balanced by the confident ones.
>
> 'Death be not proud' for example, is illuminated by the awareness of this characteristic tension. Highly rhetorical and declamatory –

Death be not proud, though some have called thee
Mighty and dreadfull, for, thou art not soe –

its tone is one of bravura rather than assurance. It blatantly travesties the character of death and the blatancy discloses an underlying hysteria. Donne first creates the illusion of death as a person: he is proud, he thinks, he tries to kill people. By pretending that death is a person Donne can believe, or appear to believe, that he dominates it. Like the dying Tamburlaine (whose words are no longer oracles), he calls death a 'slave'. But death is far more obviously a beneficiary of 'Fate, chance, kings, and desperate men' than a slave to them. And the very idea of personifying death – as unlike a living, vulnerable, and unpredictable human being as heterogeneous ideas can be – highlights the disparity between the bravurisitic view and the actuality. Elsewhere in the poem there is lame logic:

From rest and sleepe, which but thy pictures bee,
Much pleasure, then from thee, much more must flow, . . .

The strength of the 'must' draws attention to the statement's weakness. Donne presents an analogy as an argument, but analogies do not constitute arguments, they merely illustrate them. And even in terms of the analogy, this is not, as Hamlet found, the only imaginable resemblance between sleep and death.

Towards the end of the poem Donne's insecurity emerges more palpably. The question 'why swell'st thou then?' supposes that death is in fact, at this moment in the poem, assuming large proportions in Donne's own mind. And the poem ends with a theatrical gesture: 'Death thou shalt die.' But if the flourish is more than a hollow paradox, it points to the awe in which Donne still holds his subject. Had death been effectively diminished, the verb 'die' would not have seemed a strong one with which to conclude.[21]

Stachniewski goes on to suggest that Donne's fierce intellect could hardly have responded to Calvin's unchallengeable God in any other way, and, given the facts of his private life, he concludes that Donne's embracing Calvinism is entirely understandable since it proved what he felt to be true. His lived experience of frustrated ambition, and grief in losing his wife, made sense when viewed through the eyes of Calvin's ferocious God. 'He felt his dependence on God to resemble his dependence on secular patronage with its attendant frustration, humiliation and despair.'[22]

It is not at all surprising that in recent years Donne has attracted the attention of feminist critics too. The range of the love poetry in the *Songs and Sonnets*, combined with the reputation Donne has accumulated over the years, is clearly an enticement to anyone wishing to undermine what they see as a canon of literature founded on patriarchal values. In her book, *John Donne*, for the series *Writers and their Work* published by the British Council,[23] Stevie Davies divides her study very logically into three sections, the person, the male and the soul. In the first of these she immediately places her critical finger very sensitively on what attracts a lot of readers to Donne, and what has guided a lot of criticism on him:

> The language of John Donne's poetry is provocatively unique. Its singularity tempts readers to imagine that our minds are in touch and in tune with an extraordinary individual, whose speech-rhythms and tone of voice can be heard in a more abstract way, as if they rose off the page as sound-waves, to resonate in the body's as well as the mind's ear. The impression is reinforced by the dramatic situations in which the language is rooted, generating the sense of an immediate moment in a continuum of time. The blank spaces on the page before and after the event of the poem seem like a cover of white silence over the activities and circumstances which initiated and will flow out of the speech-act. We people these silent spaces with inferences deduced from the poem and in our mind's eye glimpse the shadowy 'she' or 'thou' of the woman or man addressed as a fugitive presence just beyond the margin of the book.[24]

As we have seen, many of Donne's admirers and advocates have found themselves drawn into discussion about his life, and the relationship between his work and life. Davies notes also that the difficulty in Donne seems not to inhibit this impressive energy.

The very vagaries and aberrations of this striving intelligence have a compulsive effect in begetting in a reader the sense that here, on the page, a living mind in the crises and turmoils of its life has succeeded in transferring a genuine, and somehow still-living, genetic or psychological imprint of an individual, heart and soul. In short, we feel we 'know' Donne.

That impression should not be discounted, for it records a response to a very real quality in the lyrics: an illusion of passionate and private confession which, though it has been buried between the covers of a book for over three centuries, carries a sense of the here-and-now.[25]

Davies has much of similar value to say in her first chapter. She suggests that Donne's imperative, dynamic tone is so urgent and forceful, his sense of identity so potent, that this kind of reader response is almost unavoidable. The poems dominate and provoke us via a bewildering range of rhetorical tricks, and in creating such a strong sense of authenticity, make us yearn to learn more of the man and life which bred them. But this desire is frequently baffled by the poems' own techniques which invite us to see that the figure of the poet whom we seek may well be largely our own creation. She moves on to connect Donne into the core of his age, philosophically and religiously, and provides all the accepted biographical information *en route* to an extremely lucid and illuminating exploration of grammatical difficulty. But it is her second chapter, 'The Male', which is of most interest to us here for providing a feminist view. She launchs this part of her criticism in no uncertain terms:

> Donne has been congratulated on writing on behalf of the human race. But this is an illusion. He writes as a male....Generations of critics – generally male, or women successful in the patriarchal academic world – have not only failed to locate and anatomize the problems of the sexualised vision Donne puts forward in his poetry but have actively colluded in his fantasies of omnivorous potency, preening their own maleness in the glamorized light in which he (on occasions) gilds viciousness and denies the sublimated problems which are the real and fascinating subjects of certain poems.[26]

Tracing a history of criticism which has praised Donne's masculinity, especially against the perceived femininity of earlier or even contemporary verse like Spenser's, she concentrates on Donne's misogyny in some detail:

> Much of Donne's earlier poetry specializes in obscenity. It was written by a young male bent on establishing a reputation in a male society at Lincoln's Inn, where fraternal bondings and dominance were founded on sexual prowess (whether real or feigned) of members of a predatory pack. It is not to rebuke the young poet for his supposed bad behaviour that one must stress this favour-currying machismo: rather to reproach collusive criticism for blind praise and to clarify the extent of Donne's misogyny. For traces of that misogyny, founded on fear, anger and insecurity as well as desire for approbation in a patriarchal world, are pervasive in his work. It is paradoxically an aspect of his idealism, and its psychological burdens test his trust, in the most lovely and moving of his love-poems. Misogyny grasps deep roots into the psyche that generates these poems.[27]

There follows a close analysis of a number of poems where she perceives misogyny to be the undercurrent, before she asserts:

> The stated intent of such poems is the dehumanization of woman. She becomes an edible commodity; usable goods which, when sampled, are rendered worthless; game to be flushed out and killed; a mindless piece of flesh without individuality, whose feelings are expressly not to be taken into account:[28]

Davies selects the *Elegies* for particular attention in this respect and finds numerous quotations to support her views:

> The Elegies display the male persona's potency in a series of libertine, epigrammatic, and sometimes narrative exercises written 'for the boys', each more outrageous than the last. 'The boys' are the brothel-going, cuckolding, big-talking fraternity, or at least those who exhibit themselves in those terms, and who at the same time like to identify themselves as an *avant-garde* intelligentsia. The fantasy scenarios of the Elegies convulse with lurid detail.[29]

It is interesting to compare Davies's direct approach here with

Stachniewski's anthropological time-travelling. In the grip of her own misanthropy (patriarchal uses of language are not always as exclusive as feminism assumes, so we will have to specify here that the term *excludes* women), Davies seems to forget that Donne and 'the boys' she is so eager to denigrate really were the *avant-garde* intelligentsia, as her own description of the poet in her first chapter makes eloquently clear. We might also speculate on how sensible it is to employ patriarchy as a descriptive term for Elizabethan England. To recreate Elizabeth I as some kind of masculine figure, is to underestimate deeply the religious convictions of her subjects, and especially of men like Donne, whose lives literally were dependent on the relationship between them, their God and their sovereign. Tempering this section of her essay somewhat, Davies then proceeds to suggest Donne's masculinity, as displayed in the *Elegies*, was also a way of attacking convention, and of undermining the establishment:

> These poems are generally hailed or dismissed as juicy juvenilia, praised for their intellectual brilliance and poetic panache; then subordinated to the 'great' poetry of Donne – in a sense, suppressed. But not only do they form a considerable bulk of his poetic output; they are foundation-stones for his mature poetry. Establishing an ideology, they expose the symptoms of a male aggression and exploitativeness as a mode of defiance against society as a gerontocracy, sanctioned by his peers and licensed by his dominance of wit and Ovidian shock-tactics. They attack convention as castrated and sapless, dishonourable because dishonest. The poet advertises himself as a fully equipped male. Other poets may offer compliments, flattery, sweet similitudes; he presents naked priapism and brags thereby his dangerous integrity.[30]

And Davies does not restrict her analysis of Donne's misogyny to the *Elegies* or indeed just to the secular poems. 'Contempt for women' she states, 'remains a major theme of the *Songs and Sonnets*, which span a range of amatory poetry from the salacious and abusive to the tender and the passionate'[31] before moving into analyses of the Divine Poems. In considering the well-known duality found in Donne (the proliferation of theological content in his sexual poetry, and of sexual content in his divine poetry) she finds no difficulty in being consistent about Donne's misogyny.

Such trans-sexual identification did not call for a revision of misogynistic attitudes: on the contrary, if humanity stood as female to God's male, that was because human nature incorporated all those defects Genesis and Christian tradition visited on woman: inferiority, fickleness, curiosity, and the covert itch for supremacy. There are arresting similarities between certain Divine Poems and the more salacious of his earlier erotica. The incongruous holy whore of Holy Sonnet XVIII exhibits a promiscuous ecumenism:

> Betray kind husband thy spouse to our sights,
> And let myne amorous soule court thy mild Dove,
> Who is most trew, and pleasing to thee, then
> When she'is embrac'd and open to most men.

(ll. 11–14)[32]

In chapter 3, 'The Soul', Davies rounds off her study with an examination of Donne's spirituality and internal religious turmoil as evident in the Divine Poems. She analyses several of the *Holy Sonnets* as meditations in impressive detail, and is especially interesting in her analysis of *Good Friday, 1613. Riding Westward*, which she contrasts with the sonnets and praises for its intense emotion and elusive tone.

Students of Donne looking for innovative and provocative criticism would also benefit from the collection of essays *John Donne's 'desire of more'*, edited by M. Thomas Hester.[33] Taking as the central theme the subject of Anne More in Donne's poetry, the contributors adopt extremely varied critical positions, and, on the basis of some impressively eclectic and often ingenious research, try to assess the part this enigmatic and frustratingly mute woman played in the life and work of this most absorbing of poets.

Further Reading

From the start of this book you should have gained the impression that reading the text itself, in this case Donne's poetic works, is the primary task of any student of literature. It is simply impossible to write meaningfully or effectively on any author without involving yourself deeply in a considered and thoughtful response to their work. The range and breadth of some authors' work sometimes means that, practically, students will find their studies are limited only to certain works, or groups of works, within an author's canon. This is usually the case with Donne where most students will find that the reading the *Songs and Sonnets, Satyres, Elegies* and the Divine Poems, will satisfy the demands of any academic course they may be taking. However, Donne also wrote verse letters and some individual works like *Of The Progresse of the Soule.* The definitive edition remains that edited by H.J.C. Grierson (Oxford, 1912, repr. 1979), but there is an edition of *Selected Poetry*, edited by John Hayward (Harmondsworth, 1980) which contains most of the significant poems. Helen Gardner has edited two editions of Donne's poems, *The Elegies and Songs and Sonnets* (Oxford, 1965) and *The Divine Poems* (Oxford, 1952, repr. 1978).

Prose works which may prove useful include *The Sermons of John Donne*, ed. G.R. Potter and E. M. Simpson, in 10 vols (Berkeley and Los Angeles, Calif., 1953–62), *Biathanatos*, ed. M. Rudick and M.P. Battin (New York and London, 1982), Donne's obliquely difficult defence of suicide, and *Devotions upon Emergent Occasions*, ed. J. Sparrow (Cambridge, 1923) – a second impressive collection of sermons.

The definitive biography on Donne is R.C. Bald's *John Donne: A Life* (Oxford, 1970) but *The Life and Letters of John Donne,* ed. E. Gosse, in 2 vols (London, 1899) is also a valuable biographical resource. Izaak Walton's *Life of Donne* was first published in London in 1670. A.J. Smith's book, *John Donne: The Critical Heritage* (London and Boston, Mass., 1975) is an extremely thorough and fascinating collection of critical material about Donne from the seventeenth to the end of the nineteenth century. *John Donne's Poetry,* ed. A.L. Clements (New York and London, 1966), is a very practical book because it contains both an extremely comprehensive selection of Donne's poetry and an impressive variety of critical responses from his own age to the early 1960s, with useful notes on the difficult vocabulary of the poems.

Students wishing to read more Metaphysical poetry might try verse by George Herbert, Andrew Marvell or Henry Vaughan.

Critical Texts

The critical texts referred to directly in Part II of this book are as follows:

John Carey, *John Donne: Life, Mind and Art* (London, 1981).
A.L. Clements (ed.) *John Donne's Poetry* (New York and London, 1966).
G. Hammond (ed.) *The Metaphysical Poets: A Casebook* (London, 1986).
T.S. Eliot, 'The Metaphysical Poets', *Selected Essays* (London, 1969).
C.L. Summers and T.L. Pebworth (eds.) *The Eagle and the Dove: Reassessing John Donne* (Columbia: University of Missouri Press, 1986).
John Stachniewski, *The Persecutory Imagination* (Oxford, 1991).
Stevie Davies, *John Donne* (Northcote House, Plymouth, 1994).

Of the mass of critical material available on Donne, the following is a combination of recognised and established works, and most recent studies. But just as we have recommended an informed, personal reponse to the texts throughout this book, slogging through a bibliography put together by someone else is not a very active or thoughtful way of proceeding. Searching through library shelves to locate possibly suitable works, then skimming them to decide how relevant they are for your own particular purpose, is a much more fruitful tactic. Reading the introductions to collections of essays will usually show you which essays in the book might interest you, and reading the opening sentences of each paragraph of each essay, will quickly allow you to make a similar judgement. That way you may avoid some of the criticism (all too easy to stumble on) which regards the lived experience of reading and thinking about poetry as something of an obstacle to more pressing agendas.

Alvarez, A. *The School of Donne* (New York, 1967).
Everett, Barbara *Donne: A London Poet* (Oxford, 1972).
Gardner, Helen *John Donne: A Collection of Critical Essays* (Englewood Cliffs, NJ, 1962).

Harvey, Elizabeth D. and Katherine Eisaman Maus (eds) *Soliciting Interpretation, Literary Theory and Seventeenth Century English Poetry*, (Chicago, 1990).

Hester, M. Thomas (ed.) *John Donne's 'desire of more'* (Newark and London, 1996).

Himy, Armand and Margaret Llasera (eds) *John Donne and Modernity* (Nanterre, Universite Paris X, 1995).

Leishman, J. B. *The Monarch of Wit* (New York, 1951).

Martz, Louis L. *The Poetry of Meditation* (New Haven, Conn., 1954).

Partridge, A.C. *John Donne: Language and Style* (London 1973).

Redpath, Theodore *The Songs and Sonnets of John Donne* (Methuen, London, 1983).

Smith, A.J. *John Donne: Songs and Sonets* (London, 1964).

Stein, A. *John Donne's Lyrics: The Eloquence of Action* (New York, 1980).

Tuve, Rosamund *Elizabethan and Metaphysical Imagery* (Chicago, 1947).

Notes

Chapter 1   Elegies and Lust
[1] John Carey, *John Donne: Life, Mind and Art* (London, 1981) p. 190.

Chapter 2   Satire
[1] E.M. Simpson, *A Study of the Prose Works of John Donne* (Oxford, 1948), p. 316.
[2] Carey, *John Donne*, ch. 9.

Chapter 3   The Intensity of Love
[1] Ilona Bell, "'If it be a shee': the Riddle of Donne's "Curse",' in *John Donne's "desire of more"*, edited by M. Thomas Hester, (London, 1996), p. 125.

Chapter 4   Confusion and Doubt
[1] Carey, *John Donne*, p. 232.

Chapter 5   The Poet and Mortality
[1] Carey, *John Donne*, p. 205.

Chapter 6   From Secular to Divine
[1] A.L. Clements (ed.) *John Donne's Poetry* (New York, 1966), p. 110.
[2] Carey, *John Donne*, p. 26.
[3] Germaine Greer, *Times Literary Supplement*, 24 April 1998.

Chapter 7   Divine Poetry

[1] M. Thomas Hester (ed.) *John Donne's 'desire of more'* (Newark and London, 1996), p. 9.

Chapter 8   John Donne's Life and Works

[1] Clements (ed.) *John Donne's Poetry,* p. 103.
[2] H.J.C. Grierson (ed.) *Donne, Poetical Works* (Oxford, 1977) p. xvii.
[3] Ibid., p. xvii.
[4] Carey, *John Donne*, p. 91.
[5] Clements, *John Donne's Poetry*, p. 106.

Chapter 9   The Critical History

[1] Clements, (ed.) *John Donne's Poetry*, p. 106.
[2] Samuel Johnson, *Lives of the Poets* (1779), Clements, ibid., p. 107.
[3] Ibid., pp. 107–9.
[4] G. Hammond (ed.) *The Metaphysical Poets: A Casebook* (London 1986) p. 65.
[5] Clements (ed.) *John Donne's Poetry* p. 109.
[6] Ibid., pp 109–11.
[7] T.S. Eliot, 'The Metaphysical Poets', *Selected Essays* (London, 1969) pp. 282–7.

Chapter 10   Contemporary Critical Views

[1] Carey, *John Donne*, p. 15.
[2] Ibid., p. 26.
[3] Ibid., p. 28.
[4] C.L. Summers and T.L. Pebworth (eds) *The Eagle and the Dove: Reassessing John Donne* (Columbia: University of Missouri Press, 1986), pp. 15–17.
[5] H.J.C. Grierson (ed.) *Donne: Poetical Works* (Oxford, 1977), p. xv.
[6] Ibid., pp. 193–4.
[7] In Summers and Pebworth (eds) *The Eagle and the Dove*, p. 133.
[8] Carey, *John Donne*, p. 231.
[9] Ibid., p. 261.

[10] John Stachniewski, *The Persecutory Imagination* (Oxford, 1991).
[11] Stephen Greenblatt, *Renaissance Self-Fashioning* (Chicago, 1980).
[12] Stachniewski, *The Persecutory Imagination,* p. 14
[13] Ibid., p. 14.
[14] Ibid.
[15] Ibid., p. 20.
[16] Ibid., p. 61.
[17] Ibid., p. 65.
[18] Ibid., p. 254.
[19] Ibid., p. 257.
[20] Ibid., pp. 263–4.
[21] Ibid., pp. 272–3.
[22] Ibid., p. 291.
[23] Stevie Davies, *John Donne* (Northcote House, Plymouth, 1994).
[24] Ibid., p. 1.
[25] Ibid., p. 2.
[26] Ibid., p. 30.
[27] Ibid., pp. 32–3.
[28] Ibid., p. 34.
[29] Ibid., p. 35.
[30] Ibid., pp. 36–7.
[31] Ibid., p. 39.
[32] Ibid., p. 51.
[33] Associated University Presses, London, 1996.

Index